REFLECTIONS ON
Swedish Interiors

REFLECTIONS ON
Swedish Interiors

Rhonda Eleish & Edie van Breems

Photographs by Neil Landino

Forewords by Brad Ford and Keith Granet

GIBBS SMITH
TO ENRICH AND INSPIRE HUMANKIND

First Edition
17 16 15 14 13   5 4 3 2 1

Text © 2013 Rhonda Eleish and Edie van Breems
Photographs © 2013 Neil Landino
Additional Photos
Cover, pages 4–5, 6, 10: Antiques courtesy of Dienst + Dotter Antikviteter / Jill Dienst and Daniel Dienst
Back cover, pages 8, 14: Kessler Residence / Interiors by Eleish van Breems, Ltd.
Page 2: Antiques courtesy of Tara Shaw, Inc. / Tara Shaw and Robby Walsh
Page 12: Antiques courtesy of lief / Mick Aarestrup and Paula Batali

All rights reserved. No part of this book may be reproduced by any means whatsoever without written permission from the publisher, except brief portions quoted for purpose of review.

Published by
Gibbs Smith
P.O. Box 667
Layton, Utah 84041

1.800.835.4993 orders
www.gibbs-smith.com

Designed by Sheryl Dickert
Edited by Hollie Keith
Location Production by Eleish van Breems, Ltd.
Printed and bound in Hong Kong

Gibbs Smith books are printed on paper produced from sustainable PEFC-certified forest/controlled wood source. Learn more at www.pefc.org.

Library of Congress Cataloging-in-Publication Data

Eleish, Rhonda.
  Reflections on Swedish interiors / Rhonda Eleish and Edie van Breems ;
Photographs by Neil Landino ; forewords by Brad Ford and Keith Granet. — First Edition.
       pages cm
   ISBN 978-1-4236-2528-5
 1. Interior decoration—Sweden. 2. Interior decoration—United States—
Swedish influences. I. Van Breems, Edie Bernhard. II. Title.
   NK2061.A1E425 2013
   747.09485—dc23
                              2013001386

A sofa by Danish designer Frits Henningsen (1902–1971) is shown with an eighteenth-century Swedish baroque commode, allmoge candle box and silver eighteenth-century beaker.

To my pride and joy, my daughter, Kari. —R. S. E.

With great love to my mother, Diane Ekholm Valante, who dances with the beauty of an open heart. —E. B. v. B.

Dedicated to my boys . . . my sons, Beckett and Keller. You bring a smile to my face that no words can describe. —N. L.

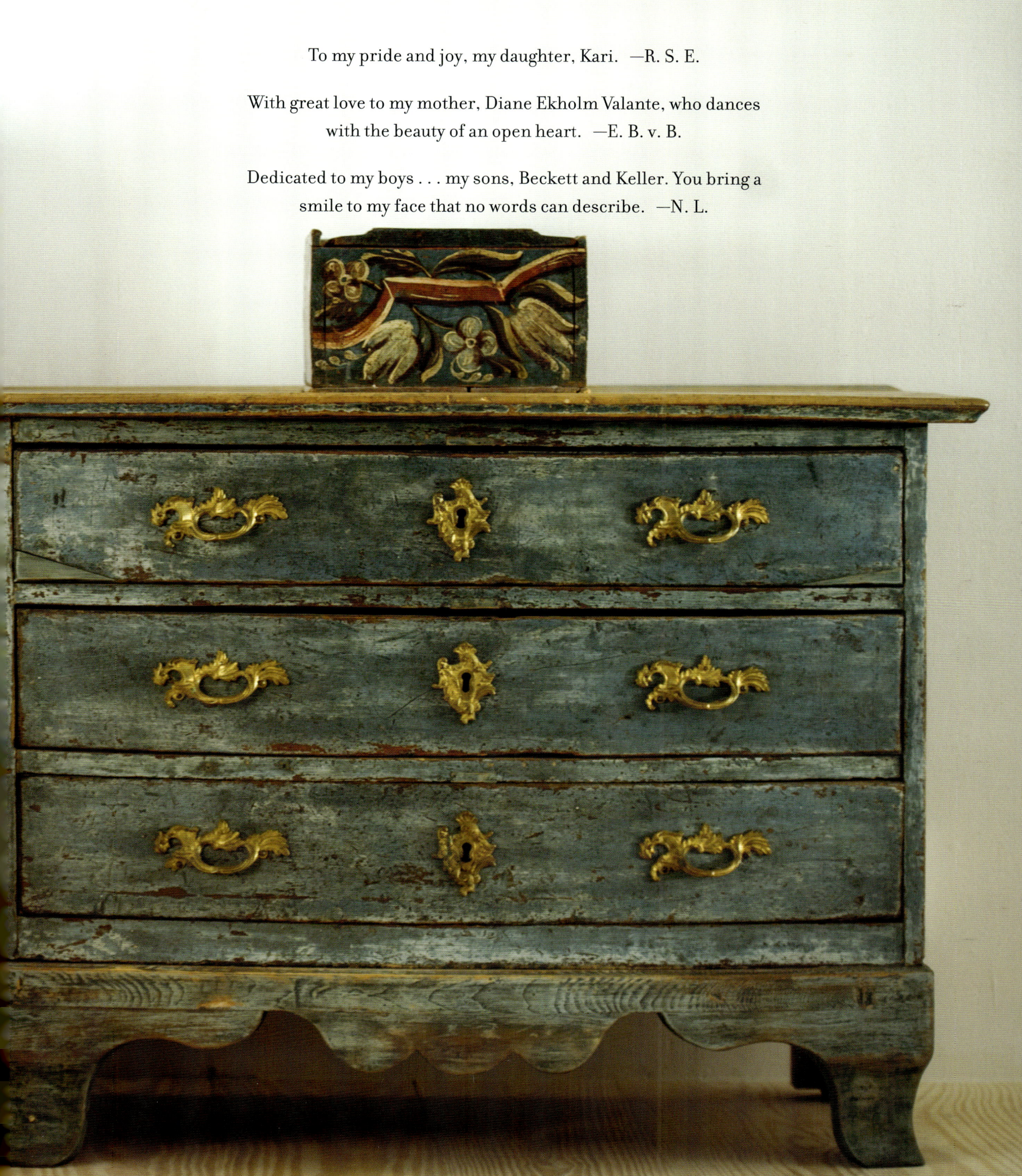

Contents

9   Foreword
by Brad Ford

11   Foreword
by Keith Granet

13   Introduction
by Edie van Breems and Rhonda Eleish

15   Graceful Living
2Michaels

41   Modern Cheer at Just Scandinavia
Ann Ljungberg and Rajesh Kumar

61   Swedish Taste at Artisan Restaurant
Rick Wahlstedt, Liza Laserow and Jonas Wickman

79   A Northern Light on the Eastern Shore
Barbara Paca and Philip Logan

101   City and Shore
Jill and Daniel Dienst

125   Romance on Duck Pond
Susan and Larry Kessler

149   Oceanside Serenity
Patricia and Jeffery Fisher

165   A Nordic Air
Ingrid Leess

181   Nordic Soul
Paula Batali and Mick Aarestrup of LIEF

207   California Calm
Linda and Lindsay Kennedy

223   Inspired Voyage
Tara Shaw

244   The Elements of Swedish Style

250   Resources

255   Acknowledgments

Foreword

BY KEITH GRANET

Arriving in Stockholm for the first time by boat from Denmark was an indelible memory for me. I was struck by the beauty of the harbor the buildings lined up like little soldiers waiting for this young man with a passion for architecture to explore. I arrived after visiting Finland and Norway, where the architecture, the colors and the light were familiar yet different. Sweden is one of those places you think about because it is always associated with beauty; it is always associated with the word *crisp*—crisp weather, crisp clean lines. For me it means natural, an appreciation for a sustainable lifestyle long before it was fashionable to even care; it seems like the Swedish people have always cared. They have always appreciated beauty in everything they do and everything they make.

When Rhonda Eleish and Edie van Breems asked me to write a foreword for their third book, *Reflections on Swedish Interiors,* I was honored, mostly because I adore these very talented women and secondly because they have become the experts to everything Swedish in the design world. Their own talents are spread across the pages of their three books along with their appreciation for the other designers, whose work are graciously displayed, communicating this beautiful, minimal, sumptuous lifestyle.

Rhonda and Edie have taught me that everything Swedish is designed yet never over-designed. The care of how a utilitarian tool looks alongside a beautifully designed piece of furniture is of equal importance. The Swedish movement has been so important to American design and *Reflections on Swedish Interiors* will continue to bring to light that importance. I know it may sound trite to say that Swedish design follows Virtruvius' three conditions of firmness, commodity and delight, but, when you look at a Swedish home or furnishing or a simple dish towel, it all carries that same level of care and comfort that makes you yearn for a home filled with these beautiful objects.

The gift that Rhonda Eleish and Edie van Breems have brought us to through their books, designs, and love of Sweden lives on in these pages and will be appreciated by all who read on.

Introduction

BY EDIE VAN BREEMS AND RHONDA ELEISH

When you walk into a good Swedish-designed room, whether it is an antique-filled country home or a contemporary industrial loft space, there is a serenity, calm and feel-good quality that literally permeates the atmosphere. Spend any amount of time in these rooms, regardless of location, and it becomes evident that Swedish interior design is not just a term—it expresses a tangible reality and a community of ideas that is no longer bound by simple nationalistic borders. Here, we share and reflect on how some of the most authentic advocates of Swedish design working in America, many of them Swedes, are using these ideas in their own homes, places of pure beauty and simplicity. The fundamental concepts of Swedish design are in full play here and are the qualities we always make a priority of incorporating into our own design work for clients—those of functionality, quality of materials, light, preservation, art, eclecticism, color, sense of place and a deep reverence for nature.

Our two previous books, Swedish Interiors and Swedish Country Interiors, took a more academic approach, discussing at some length the origins of Swedish furnishings and design philosophy. Scandinavian design has since been embraced globally and has permeated into our American consciousness in ways we had not imagined as our own notions of lifestyle and eco-consciousness grow closer to those of the Swedes. We are excited to present this new book as a touchstone and compendium of pure visual inspirations and concepts with wonderful commentary from some of our dearest and most admired friends and colleagues. By gathering and holding a mirror to these concepts in this book, we invite you to reflect, dream and perchance steal some of their magic for your own home, purpose and happiness.

As they say in Sweden—Good Design for Everybody!

—Edie & Rhonda

Graceful Living

2 MICHAELS

Twin sisters Jayne and Joan Michaels are the principals of the New York–based design firm 2Michaels, and are long-time advocates of Scandinavian design. Their studies of Scandinavian design masters have left a lasting impression much in evidence in their approach to their work. Quite simply, Jayne states, "The unsung hero is how deceptively simple Swedish design looks. Yet it's utterly complex. To me that's genius."

Jayne described their early influences: "We lived in Palm Springs, California, from the age of eleven through eighteen. The desert landscape was pure and graphic, the clarity of light vivid and strong, and the houses were low and modern. Joan and I then lived in Italy from the age of twenty-two to twenty-six. In Milan, we became friends with Franco Albini's son Marco and ended up living in a Franco Albini–designed apartment building. During that period, I discovered the work of Franco Albini, Gio Ponti, Caccia Dominioni, Carlo Scarpa, and Carlo Mollino."

"Then, I moved on to the Scandinavian architects and designers such as Alvar Aalto, Finn Juhl, Gunnar Asplund Märta Måås-Fjetterström, Carl Malmsten and Kerstin Horlin Holmquist, Carl Harry Stålhane, Berndt Friberg, etc. I was highly influenced by Swedish interior design books. I was drawn to the quiet refinement of the rooms and the quality of light." So inspired was Jayne that when she designed her apartment, she chose a Swedish palette—parchment, silver, slate, celadon, ochre and teal—furnishing the rooms with Swedish rugs and Scandinavian furniture and pottery. Asking what Jayne thinks of when she thinks of Sweden, her response is, "Pure, simple, light, fresh, refined."

Jayne's sister Joan, and other half of the design duo, is equally passionate about Scandinavian design, particularly the rugs by Marta Mass-Fjetterstrom. "I love the subtlety of the color palette. The smudgy blues, ochres, silvery greens and toasty browns. They are warm and cool, soft and strong. Josef Frank is another favorite of mine. His pieces are

Clean, fluid lines of the fruit wood side table are Italian in design, yet sit well in Scandinavian-inspired interiors that are focused on a paring down of design and form.

swing a chandelier

LEFT: Mid-twentieth-century Finnish dining table and Danish chairs sit at the heart of the dining room. The Apparatus chandelier creates an airy whimsy to the light-filled space. Vintage dining chairs, whose sleek forms are based on traditional Swedish farm chairs, surround a modernist dining table.

BELOW: This closeup shows detail of the Apparatus chandelier by Apparatus Studio.

When asked who her unsung hero is of Swedish design, Joan replies, "Kerstin Horlin Holmquist. Look up the Garden of Eden chaise lounge or anything from the Garden of Eden series. The shapes are so quirky. They remind me a bit of Carlo Mollino; sculptural and sensuous."

timeless." When questioned about which words come to mind when she thinks of Sweden, Joan replies, "elegant, spare, quiet, relaxed and clean."

Joan also remembers fondly living in Milan, Italy, during the late eighties. "We were lucky enough to live in a Franco Albini–designed building furnished with his pieces. His sensibility is similar to Swedish design in that it is spare, almost floaty, and elegant. It was an incredible education in design."

"The Abington," a 1905 newly restored, Georgian-style building in New York's West Village (a former nursing home, and prior to that, a hotel) was a project close to 2Michael's heart. When commissioned to design the model apartment for the historic building, 2Michaels referred back to the sisters' love of Scandinavian design and color palate as the basis. From that, additional hues were blended into their artful mix, which included, among others, the Italian design masters they had first discovered in Milan. As a result, a merging of lived experiences and inspirations created a space that is fresh, chic and inviting.

FACING: Contemporary artist Hermione Ford's "Untitled, 2010," is featured in the living room supported by works of Scandinavian design greats Holmquist and Malmsten, to name a few.

The Kerstin Horlin Holmquist–designed chair evokes beautiful simplicity and remains timeless in form.

RIGHT: Subdued legs with the slightest of curve add a subtle dimension to the overall brilliance of the design.

According to Jayne, "I love the timeless beauty of Swedish design; the quiet grace. Holmquist comes to mind. The gentle curve of the back in the sofa, the splay of the leg, there's a neoclassical elegance even though it was designed in 1960."

Ten days spent in Sweden left a lasting impression on Joan. "I was visiting an artist friend. It was in June and the weather couldn't have been more perfect. It was crystal clear and sparkling. I spent most of the day outdoors. It was light until almost nine or ten. The people on the street and in the cafes seemed so happy. I remember eating a lot of salmon with dill, yellow potatoes, multigrain bread with delicious cheeses. Everything was clean, light and healthy".

The side table by Swiss company Embru, ca. 1940s, is featured in the corner of the living room, and the painting nearby is by contemporary German artist Karl Klingbiel. The painting on the window wall is by contemporary Australian artist Timothy Paul Myers.

The collection of pottery on display is by Scandinavian potters Stålhane, Palshus, Lindberg, and Rorstrand.

According to Jayne, "I'd have to say we create a sense of serenity in our projects, we tend to use blues, greens and fresh colors, and we also use Swedish and Italian mid-century furniture."

find a balance

Silk stripes replace traditional cotton ticking used on eighteenth- and nineteenth-century Scandinavian antiques, reflecting the formality and glamour of the 1940s. A canned settee by Swedish master designer Carl Malmsten (1888–1972), ca. 1940, floats center in the living room. Behind the settee is a rare coffee table by mid-century Brazilian designer Sergio Rodrigues (1927), and a Tomlinson slipper chair.

LEFT: A Kerstin Horlin Holmquist, ca. 1950, lays center field in the master bedroom. The tonal hues of blue and grey, pickled floors and putty custom mohair rug are soothing components of Scandinavian design. A Gio Ponti, ca. 1940, headboard in walnut contributes a warm tone, which complements the adjacent side table.

ABOVE: A pair of Uovo chairs attributed to Italian designer Ico Parisi (1916–1996) floats effortlessly in the master bedroom.

Graceful Living | 27

"Swedish design looks deceptively simple. Yet it's utterly complex. To me that's genius."

FACING: Shown is a traditional design detail, updated by Swedish master designer Kerstin Horlin Holmquist, ca. 1950.

THIS PAGE: Italian master designer Gio Ponti's side table, ca. 1950s, is featured with a work by American contemporary photographer Frank Veteran.

A Gio Ponti Tea Set, ca. 1930s, is perfectly displayed on a sculpturally based, glass-top side table.

BELOW: A rare custom walnut vanity by Ico Parisi, ca. 1952, and chair complete the master bedroom. The blue-grey tone of the upholstered velvet complements the tonal blues in the room.

RIGHT: For the master bedroom, Joan and Jayne chose a walnut headboard by renowned designer Gio Ponti, ca. 1940..

The installation art on display is by contemporary Australian artist Timothy Paul Myers. It is made up of intricate geometric patterns of pencil stubs on baseball cards.

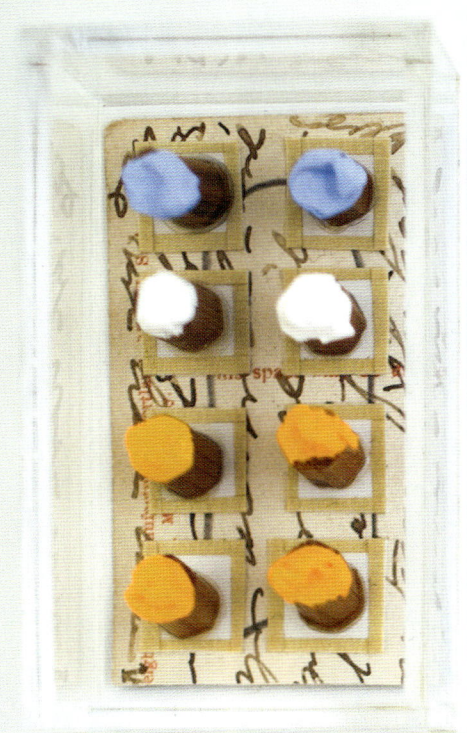
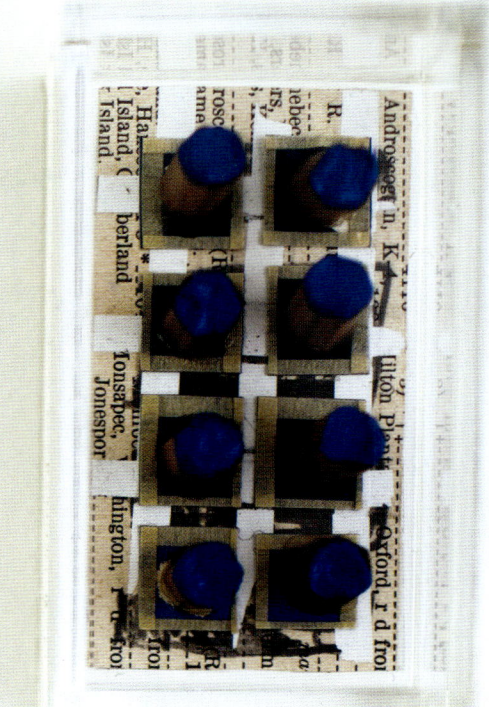
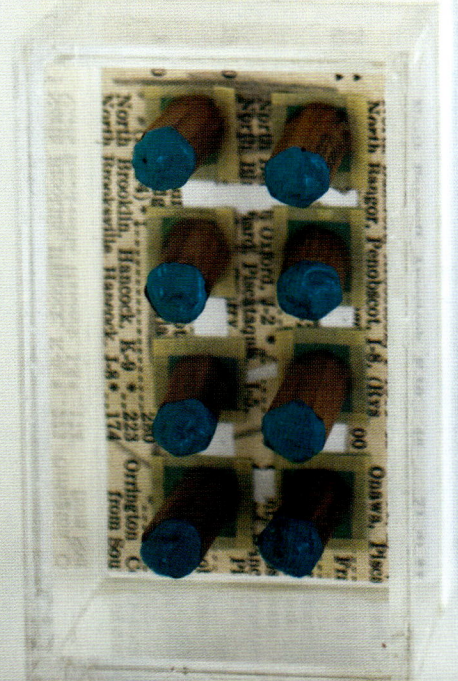

LEFT: A 1950s walnut desk hovers on the rug of the rug in the study, anchored by an arm chair, ca. 1951, by Italian designer Carlo DiCarli (1910–1971).

FACING: A view of Italian designer Franco Albini's (1905–1997) arm chair, ca. 1940s, in the office.

rich leather

Works of contemporary German artist Peter Buechler hang over a red leather sofa from the 1950s by Danish designer Borge Mogensen (1914–1972).

ABOVE: On display, a mobile attributed to master American designer Charles Eames (1907–1978). Charles Eames was highly influenced by the Finnish architect Eliel Saarinen. Eliel's son Eero, also an architect, became a partner and friend to Eames. Eames dedicated what was to become his famous "Eero" chair to Eliel.

FACING: Jayne and Joan loved the play of shapes and richness of the wood on this mobile attributed to Charles Eames.

Modern Cheer at Just Scandinavia

ANN LJUNGBERG AND RAJESH KUMAR

Ann Ljungberg is passionate about the things in life that matter. In design she declares that these are books, fabrics and a comfortable sofa with a high back to share with a good friend, which may be a book, your spouse or even your best friend from high school. Simple and true advice always—this is what we love and admire in our friend Ann. When it comes to home design, she and her partner, Rajesh Kumar, can be found enthusiastically sharing with all the practical joys of Scandinavian modernism and contemporary design through their company Just Scandinavian. Based in New York, Just Scandinavian is the place to call for fresh, vibrant Swedish fabric designs from Svenskt Tenn to newly manufactured lamps and chairs by venerable names such as Finn Juhl, Bruno Mathsson International, and newer ones such as Zweed by Håken Johansson. Ann's well-curated collection comes from her commitment to bringing the highest-quality Scandinavian design to America. Starting with the Stockholm Exhibition in 1939, Sweden went through a radical shift of focus onto well-made manufactured furniture, preferably with materials found in native Scandinavia. Still manufactured in Scandinavia by top design houses, many of these designs have become part of the canon of great twentieth century furniture and Ann and Rajesh are at the forefront of making them available to a new audience of Americans for the new century.

Ann credits her eye for exceptional art and furniture on looking and touching, skills she acquired not just on the job as a Stockholm antiques dealer, but from her grandmother while growing up. "I always loved linen and painted furniture," says Ann, "and always appreciated the details you find in older pieces of furniture, even the simple, far from fancy pieces. Quality does not always equal high price." In her home, as in her store, the focus is on comfortable furniture, light wood, bright white and added colors through textiles. "What I love the most about Swedish design is the love for light in the

Ann mixes high and low traditional Swedish forms such a Gustavian-style dining table, Asplund shelving unit and Ant Chairs with grace and confidence. Collections of books and china are attractively stacked and left in full view for ease for use and accessibility. The silver coffee set was from a dear friend of Ann's aunt and uncle, Roy Urban, a Stockholm silvermaker during the 1960s.

house created by white or bright colors on the walls and floors, by light window treatments, by streamlined lamps. This to me is what we mean by Scandinavian simple style—not sleek in design with no detail; that is a misperception—what is meant, is keeping all things simple." Ann muses that there is perhaps something in the psyche of all Scandinavians that lends to this focus on simple orderly design. "It is incredible actually. From the vast, dark green forests in the north of Sweden with endless miles of empty roads, all the way down to the flat fields in the south of Skåne and Denmark, where there are small villages with white churches every second intersection, everywhere it is pretty, you rarely see big industrial areas with smoking chimneys. Everywhere you travel, you will find it so neat and almost arranged."

To enter Ann and Rajesh's apartment is to release any preconceived notions one may have that Swedish simplicity is an austere and unforgiving style, only for the disciplined few. Their Manhattan living room commands a bird's soaring view of the Hudson River and light from a bank of picture windows floods onto a large wall covered in a riot of cheerful, bright yellow, green and blue botanical wallpaper by Josef Frank for Svenskt Tenn. A whimsical Ox chair by Hans Wegner commands the living room with its giant headrest horns and a very personal collection of Ann and Rajesh's family photos and Swedish antiques are arranged artfully with the modern furniture. The overall impression is sophisticated, sparse without being spare, fresh, light, balanced and uplifting.

The stars here really are the Josef Frank textiles, furniture and light fixtures; all from Svenskt Tenn. "He was such a genius," marvels Ann, "with over two hundred textile and a thousand furniture designs." An Austrian-born designer and architect, Josef Frank started his career during a period in the early twentieth century when there were great debates

"I look back to my childhood," says Ann, "when I was in the midst of my family with grandparents, cousins and lots of people and Sweden was very prosperous and full of hope for the future. It was an idyll and I remember the light hitting my grandmother's spoon for powdered sugar in silver. Us kids were allowed to take as much sugar as we wanted to our strawberries with milk! That feeling of joy and freedom and beauty is what I often come back to when I think of Sweden."

The daybed in the guest room is from Tempur in Sweden.

mix old

44 | Modern Cheer at Just Scandinavia

and new

FACING: The white Karin chair by Bruno Mathsson for Dux in the 1970s faces a limestone coffee table by G.A.D. of Gotland. The photos on the wall are of Ann's mother and aunt when they were seven or eight years old that Ann had blown up and framed. The Paradise wallpaper adds a fantastic glow to the room during sunsets. "Having white walls with just photos and paintings on it we found was a bit too harsh with all the light from the windows," says Ann. "The wallpaper helps to give more of a warmth to the room and embraces the seating area and sets it off for the other corners in this pretty open area."

ABOVE: The Danish Ox chair is the undisputed star of the living room. The Ox was a favorite of Hans Wegner's own designs and was based upon his fascination with Picasso. Wegner, like his Scandinavian contemporaries, was focused on organic functionality, but the true success of the Ox chair lies in its subtle humor.

The wallpaper, called Paradiset White, is one of six wallpapers designed by Josef Frank for Svenskt Tenn in the 1940s.

going on regarding the philosophy of modern living. Frank gradually moved away from the strict functionalism of Corbusier and the Bauhaus to embrace his own form of a more organic functionalism with a focus on textiles and upholstered furniture with an emphasis on plant forms and bright colors. During the political and racial oppression of the war years, Frank and his Swedish wife lived in Sweden and New York, and Frank began his long partnership with the Swedish design company Svenskt Tenn, for which he is famous. His exuberant forms based on nature, fused with Frank's interest in the totality of the home environment as a functional whole, resonated deeply with Swedes' own love of nature and rich tradition of functional decorative arts.

Rajesh was not initially familiar with Frank's designs but fell in love with them, choosing the wallpaper named Paradise for the living room. From India, where the decorative arts are colorful and exuberant, Rajesh says that at first not all of Swedish modern excited him but that he has since been totally won over. "I started to really feel the quality and got very interested. The design standard in Sweden is so much higher than in both India and the United States in general. For example, we renovated Ann's summerhouse this spring and the construction workers took away the upper parts of the floor. The wood under that was as good as new and the house is from 1902! I feel safe in Sweden. There is a way of living there that is very neat, sound and clean in all of its design."

Anchoring one corner of the room is a still life of an eighteenth-century Swedish pewter tankard and pear painting by a local New York artist on a Swedish antique tilt-top alder root table from 1790. A seeming riot of colors and patterns, the combination of the Svenskt Tenn fabrics and wallpaper in Ann and Rajesh's living room work together with white, spring green and nautical blue being their uniting bond.

FACING: Bringing unexpected warmth to a room, the bioethanol flame wall fireplace by Kjell Thompsen hangs over a Josef Frank–designed desk and chair. Hurricane oil lanterns by Arne Jacobsen for Stelton stand at the ready to be lit.

BELOW: Ann says that this is one of the most popular chairs she sells and is one of the few she has by a Norwegian designer. It is called Scandia and was made by Hans Brattrud in 1957 and has been in production by Fjordfiesta ever since.

flora

suecia

The bedroom is a soothing retreat all in white highlighted with punches of cheery Josef Frank fabric and a traditional blue-and-white gingham Gripsholm armchair.

bold color

The ideal of well-designed, beautiful, harmonious interiors achieved by Frank and his contemporaries still holds a powerful allure for Ann. "What I miss in the design climate of today is some ideas/ideals of how a home should look and how it should be used. Designers of today just make a lamp of a ballerina skirt, some pots of birch wood, a chair that looks like a tennis racket. I would like to gather the new designers and ask them: What are you thinking of? Do you have any ideas of context? In the fifties and sixties in Sweden a bunch of surveys and investigations were made of how many steps a housewife made on a normal day, how many towels she needed, how you could reduce the number of plates and platters for making things easier for her. What happened? Today we live in a more global world, a lot more ways of living a life is accepted and perhaps it is too much going on even for the designers." And to this Ann presents a challenge for every burgeoning contemporary functionalist to rise to. "I hope the designers soon start to tell us how we should try to live decent lives in a world with problems like overpopulation and big environmental issues that need to be solved. What are they waiting for?"

Colorful rolls of textiles line the walls at Just Scandinavia.

A delicate lighting fixture by Josef Frank with elephant shades.

Ann called the manufacturer in Denmark of the Hans Wegner Wishbone chair to see if they would paint it in turquoise for her. She has started a trend and now and the company is painting the chairs in other bright colors. "I hope Hans Wegner won't mind," laughs Ann.

"When I think of Swedish design, I see Falu Rödfärg or Falun Red. That color," explains Ann, "is a product derived from producing copper (environmentally correct from the thirteenth century!). It preserves wood and adds color. All over Sweden it is the most common color of any wooden building and goes so well with the green color of the pine forests. Perfect harmony between nature and man!"

Here is the so-called Banana Couch by Josef Frank, upholstered in one of Frank's later fabrics called Ceylon. Hanging above the couch on the wall is a rug designed by Pia Wallén for Asplund in Stockholm.

"He must have been one of the most productive geniuses there was in the home designing business… when will the next Mr. Frank appear?"

ABOVE: Josef Frank based this cabinet on a sketch he had made called "cabinet with 21 drawers," although there are only nineteen drawers on the finished cabinet. The cabinet is made with Wawona root veneer and walnut.

FACING: The brass hardware on Josef Frank's Cabinet with Twenty One Drawers is of all different sizes.

Swedish Taste at Artisan Restaurant

RICK WAHLSTEDT, LIZA LASEROW AND JONAS WICKMAN

Rick Wahlstedt, a successful restaurateur, drew upon Swedish farmhouse designs from his homeland as well as his own refined vision of the classic Swedish husmanskost bistro when creating Artisan at the Delamar Hotel in Southport, Connecticut. Already having restaurants in New York City, Chicago, Las Vegas, Miami, Atlanta with designs that vary from French Colonial 1920 to contemporary Japanese Kyoto 1960, Rick comments that "Artisan is not the first restaurant but the one that is the closest to my heart due to my Swedish heritage. The story that I really wanted to tell was that of a chic New England bed and breakfast with classic Swedish bones juxtaposed with a certain unexpected contemporary element." Championing the New England farm-to-table movement, Artisan's dining room needed to be atmospheric while keeping the focus on the food. Coming directly from the farms and fisherman in the surrounding area, the food, as conceived by French Executive Chef Frederic Kieffer, is fresh and complex. To show off the cuisine to best effect, Rick understood that the balance between subtlety and strength in décor had to be just right.

The monumental flower murals of renowned Stockholm artist Jonas Wickman caught Rick's eye and in these he felt he had found the perfectly bold understatement for Artisan's dining room. A favorite of arts patrons such as H&M founder Stefan Persson and Time Warner's Alex Vik, Jonas's work ranges from exacting Gustavian eighteenth-century palace-style murals to muted, hazy landscape paintings and portraits. "What I thought was interesting was how diversified Jonas is with his art," recalls Rick of his first impressions of the artist. "He can paint in a very contemporary style or classic landscapes or even abstract. Few painters have that range of knowledge and depth and, after speaking to him over the phone regarding his enthusiasm about the project as I outlined it to him, I became reassured that we could work together to create something unexpected on the two large walls." The pair agreed for Jonas to paint a giant white tulip

A delicate nest-shaped chandelier of copper defines the private dining room at Artisan. Light streams through sheer linen curtains, illuminating the magnolia mural by Stockholm artist Jonas Wickman. Bellman-style chairs, upholstered in soft yellow and white gingham surround a Gustavian-style dining table.

"A Swedish tile stove is such a cozy thing to have…both efficient and beautiful."

for Artisan's tavern room and a twisting attenuated Magnolia branch with buds on the cusp of blossoming. The two flower murals bring nature inside, gently and effectively reminding diners of Artisan's fresh from nature approach to cuisine.

An international antiques dealer and interior designer, with stores in Manhattan and Southern Sweden, Lisa Laserow became involved in the middle of the creation of Artisan as Rick was sourcing furniture. Rick found that Liza, originally from the south of Sweden, was the missing link to tie everything together. "She grasped the project immediately and we saw most things the same way. Liza had a great vision for the garden and pergola outside and she is bold with her color schemes as well as fabric combinations, which makes the whole thing fresh and chic as supposed to old and stuffy. Being both of Swedish ancestry helped us to understand one another and I could not be more pleased with our collaboration." Liza agrees that sharing a Swedish background with Rick and Jonas helped to make the project seamless.

"Let's just say that "State of Mind is Swedish Design," says Liza with a smile, when describing her design collaboration with Rick and Jonas on Artisan and what distinguishes a Swedish interior. "Simple structure is really the way a Swede dwells. You have what you need. In order to achieve this simplicity in my interiors, I like to first start by stripping everything down. Essentially, building the space from nothing, adding layers and only at the last I finish with the details." In the restaurant this was done by spending significant time getting the flooring, lighting and walls just right and of the highest quality to Liza's exacting standards. The walls, for example, have almost a velvet glazing, a luxurious detail insisted upon by Liza. The floor was lime-washed with a traditional scrub, hand mixed and colored by Jonas. All the chairs were hand painted and waxed by Liza's faux finishers in many layers to give an aged richness of patina. "All the details, even the hardware, had to be really clean," says Liza. "This allows the extravagant elements to speak in the serenity of the space."

Those extravagant yet refined elements are scattered throughout the restaurant's several distinct seating areas and reveal themselves slowly as one walks through the restau-

Classic Gripsholm-style sofas and chairs are grouped for casual conversation around the Swedish kakelugn that Rick Wahlstedt had imported from Sweden expressly for Artisan's tavern room.

Swedish Taste at Artisan Restaurant | 63

rant. The lush oversized wall murals of tulips and blossoming magnolia branches by Jonas cover the walls, their luminous white colors offset by the olive grey wall colors. Custom-made sculptural copper contemporary chandeliers, evoking bird nests, hang in the private dining room and at a banquette. The focal point of the Tavern room is a massive pewter Parisian bar that one would not be surprised to find visited by the likes of Hemingway and Fitzgerald exchanging bon mots.

Dominating another seating area in the tavern room, and defining the mood as totally Scandinavian, is a white Swedish kakelugn, or tile stove, imported by Rick to be the jewel of the restaurant. The glowing fire of the stove is an inviting spot for guests to gather, and to that end, Liza installed groupings of comfortable Gripsholm armchairs and sofas around the stove. The Gripsholm furniture is an eighteenth-century form traditionally found in many country homes in Sweden, as is the tile stove. "A tile stove is such a cozy thing to have. In Sweden, if you are building a house in the country, it is both efficient and beautiful," says Liza.

The outdoor seating area, designed by Liza, is meant to be used almost year-round and employs comfortable lounge chairs and heat lamps surrounding a central tree. More formal dining tables are lit by lanterns and mason jar

BELOW: In an homage to Swedish glassware, hand-blown custom glass pendants illuminate the pewter-topped Parisian bar. The panes of the French doors are playfully reflected in the moss green globes.

FACING: Artisan's food is based on Husmanskost, the simple traditional food of the Swedish countryside, typified by local seasonal ingredients. One of Artisan's signature desserts is Fluffy Vanilla Cheesecake with Fresh Blueberry Marmalade.

A favorite seating area is a round table next to the bookcase, where a collection of eighteenth-century Swedish books, boxes, brass and glassware are on display. "I wanted it to feel as if you were dining in someone's living room," says Liza of installing the large black bookcase.

A metal wall made with panels of antiqued mirrored glass divides the dining room from the tavern room at Artisan. The pine floors were first scrubbed and mellowed with a special limewash created by artist Jonas Wickman.

All of the metal hardware in the restaurant, including the iron sconces, were meticulously chosen for their strong character and refinement.

"Let's just say that Swedish design is a state of mind . . ."

pendants hanging from a covered pergola near a large welcoming bar. In a hospitable European detail, blankets with Artisan's logo are provided to guests on chilly nights. The overall impression is of elegance, serenity and balance; all being hallmarks of great Swedish design.

Since opening, Artisan has been a huge success, garnering rave reviews for food and décor. "The best work," says Rick, "comes from collaboration with talented people who can stay within the intent of a project but bring a slight edge to it in a convincing way and Jonas and Liza did just that! I am pleased. My four goals are great room, great food, good and friendly service, and good value. I think Artisan meets those expectations and my hope is that it will be a home for our clients for many, many years to come!"

FACING: The beauty of the private dining room is in its simplicity. The floor boards, the muted color scheme, the punctuation of the fresh spring green in the murals and floral arrangement all work together to create a soothing dining space.

BELOW: In keeping with Executive Chef Frederic Kieffer's farm-to-table cuisine, seasonal flowers grace each table. The china and stemware were chosen for their simplicity, enabling the food to be the focus of the meal.

bring the outdoors in

FACING: A favorite gathering place is the outdoor bar and dining area on the terrace. Liza designed the custom lanterns for the entrance and seating area.

Spring White and Green Asparagus with Seared Atlantic Salmon and Mushroom

FACING: A special shutter system was made to be able to close the bar when not in use. Here is a wonderful example of Swedish attention to making something purely functional and beautiful in its own right.

ABOVE: The Artisan logo was designed by Fabian Berglund.

RIGHT: The reflection of mason jar light pendants sparkle like fireflies in the mirror hung on the exterior wall of the restaurant. Blankets such as they have in Sweden are provided for diners to enjoy their meal alfresco, even on a cool evening.

use the unexpected

BELOW: The outdoor dining room is a lush green oasis as viewed from the courtyard at the Delamar Hotel.

FACING: The mason jar pendant lamps were custom designed by Liza Laserow and are a great example of the use of recycled materials and unexpected whimsy. The pergola ceiling is covered in rattan shades to filter the light.

A Northern Light on the Eastern Shore

BARBARA PACA AND PHILIP LOGAN

Barbara Paca's work as an international landscape architect is informed by her deep love of the history of botanical exploration as well as an abiding respect for the architectural traditions of her eighteenth-century Maryland ancestors. The tidal inlets, waterways and rolling farmland of Maryland's Eastern Shore run in her veins, and it is here that she and her husband, Philip Logan, have put down roots in the form of a nineteenth-century house in the peaceful and historic village of Oxford. Barbara and Philip's New York–based company, Preservation Green, LLC, also maintains a private satellite in Oxford where the focus is on developing sustainable alternatives to the way buildings and landscapes are made.

Taking us through her garden, Barbara explains her admiration for early American and Swedish design. "There is a deep reverence for Mother Nature inherent in both styles of architecture that Philip and I embrace. Like early Swedish architecture, early American architecture had to tip its hat to the formidable forces of a new world. As our *weltanschauung,* or world view, is sharpened vis-à-vis the fragility of the environment, many of us are returning to traditional common sense principles in the way we design and live in nature." The renovations and additions to the house, as viewed from the garden, are a testament to Barbara and Philip's vision of living in harmony with their geographic location. Exterior balconies and decks were added to increase the connection to the outside and allow for more light and air into the house. The house was made more accessible for their son Tilghman, who is wheelchair bound, by adding a ramp and an interior elevator to access all three floors. Modern technologies were added to decrease the carbon footprint, such as transitioning to a geothermal system and integrating German solar panels.

A Swedish Rococo stool and Gustavian armchairs that Barbara brought home from Paris started her well-curated Swedish antiques collection. A landscape architect, Barbara was immediately taken by the grey-painted eighteenth-century Swedish architect's desk.

The studio, built by Barbara and Philip as homage to Maryland's Wye House Orangerie, is lit at night by chandeliers from Prague, found in an old house on the Tred Avon River. Urns from an overgrown garden near Baltimore are set on top of the massive rococo stove from Switzerland.

"When I think of Sweden . . . Carl Linnaeus! Carl Linnaeus was a genius. I couldn't hope to hold a candle to his legacy. I just admire the way he saw the world around him, took it in, and reinterpreted it to others with brilliance and good taste. Hammarby is a dream, and in that vision are all of the elements that changed and conquered the natural world."

Barbara and Philip's regard for practical yet sophisticated designs from the past are visible in the new studio addition filled with Swedish Gustavian antiques. Traditional black-and-white marble tiles set on the diagonal run the length of the two-story room flanked by jib doors which open dramatically onto the back garden, pool and a small hunting lodge, called the Gunnery. The studio is inspired by the Orangerie at Wye House, the oldest existing greenhouse in America and one of Barbara's favorite buildings of the world. "Wye's orangerie served as a beautiful laboratory where great botanical experiments were conducted," says Barbara, "We were deeply inspired by the high artistic and engineering achievements of that mid-eighteenth-century space." A large Baroque tile stove, ca. 1730, is the focal point of the studio space. Imported from Switzerland, it was reassembled by American and Austrian craftsmen using modern firebrick and mortar. The incredibly efficient radiant heating system of the kakelugn, traditional to Swedish and Northern European homes, made sense from a practical as well as visual point of view. "Americans tend to rely on woodstoves more than kachelofens. Could it be that Europeans are more family oriented and as a result they plan for subsequent generations? Once Americans realize how much nicer and more energy efficient it is to have a gentle, radiant heat (versus the burning hot surfaces of a Jøtul or Fisher stove), I think they will lean toward kachelofens. Wood is, after all, a renewable resource and Americans have been conquering their forests for centuries to make room for farmland!"

Using what is natively available and repurposing materials is an aspect of early Swedish and American design bred from necessity. It also often came from a deep pride of place when landowners would build using the very best materials their holdings offered. At Preservation Green, Philip explains that they are committed to the use of

When building the studio, black-and-white marble tile flooring was installed. The tile flooring is a sly nod to the northern palaces of Europe and a natural backdrop for Barbara's fine collection of Swedish Gustavian antiques. Black-and-white marble tiles were also traditionally used in many gracious early American homes for their durability and good effect. The jib doors are signature to early Maryland houses; evidence of Marylanders' love of the outdoors and strong aesthetic desire to blur the line between inside and exterior space. The pale robin's-egg-blue tea table is Gustavian, ca. 1780.

reclaimed materials, such as the painted pine railings and doors they salvaged from Plimhimmon, one of the ancestral homes of the Tilghman family. "The combination of materials in their raw state, expressed functionality and the celebrations of the effects of time results in a patina that is textured and historic without becoming a pastiche. These surfaces cannot be re-created but only allowed to breathe with new life in the simple fresh compositions we are able to create." Reclaimed heart pine cut from Baltimore warehouse beams was used for flooring and four-inch-thick marble slabs from Independence Mall in downtown Philadelphia surround the therapy pool in the garden. Architectural integrity was preserved wherever possible in the house, with all of the windows completely taken apart and cleaned of old lead paint, gently whitewashed and sealed with safe products. Native plants are also a big part of the "using the best of what is already there" equation. "One of my favorite plants," says Barbara, "is the bright yellow Black Eyed Susan, scientific name *Rudbeckia hirta*. The State Flower of Maryland, this treasure provides nectar to nourish butterflies and seeds that feed birds during the winter months. Appropriately, Carl Linnaeus named this American beauty Rudbeckia in honor of his professor, Olaf Rudbeck. I like mixing Rudbeckia with three cultivars of the very native Maryland flowering tobacco; namely, the tall muscular *Nicotiana sylvestris,* green *Nicotiana langsdorfii* and my favorite, the fragrant *Nicotiana affinis*. My passion for blending New and Old World plants is probably the greatest driving force behind my work as a landscape designer."

Barbara's love of the Swedish Baroque and Rococo periods, as well as the Gustavian, are deeply personal. Her family is among the first colonial settlers with many distinguished relatives, among them William Paca who was a signer of the Declaration of Independence. Paca and his family were painted by the famous Charles Willson Peale, who was educated in the tradition of the important Swedish portraitist

FACING: A Gustavian crystal chandelier hangs above an arrangement of Nicotiana 'White Perfume'—adored for being at its most fragrant on hot summer nights.

ABOVE: A view from the studio looks out upon the Gunnery, Barbara's twin brother, Dr. Robert Paca's hunting lodge. A rococo Swedish settee is set out under the Gunnery arbor on sunny days.

"Americans will come to realize how much nicer and more energy efficient it is to have a gentle, radiant heat."

Gustavus Hesselius (1682–1755) and his son John Hesselius. His relations were painted by the Hesselius family on many occasions. Paca's interest in these Swedish family portraits, as well as with famous Swedish botanist Carl Linnaeus, meant she was poised and curious when Swedish antiques crossed her path one winter afternoon in Paris. Collecting, Barbara was soon to learn, can start as a fascination and become a fate. When Barbara contacted us at Eleish van Breems, Ltd, to locate specific pieces and help her curate her expanding collection, we were delighted to guide her. It has been a privilege over the years to watch Barbara skillfully integrate special eighteenth-century Swedish furniture into her Maryland home and other projects. From a built-in country stuga-style bed to a fine collection of gilt mirrors, each piece is showcased thoughtfully and to great effect. "Swedish antiques were an integral part of the renovation." Barbara relates, "And I relied on my trusted experts, Rhonda and Edie, to allow me to purchase worthy pieces around which spaces were created. The blending of Swedish and American eighteenth-century furniture and decorative arts sits well in a place as remote and romantic as Maryland's Eastern Shore."

Barbara and Philip are next combining their skills and creativity to transform a commercial property in Oxford, once owned by one of the founding African American families of Maryland's Eastern Shore, into a state-of-the-art horticultural research center. "Like our home," says Philip, "the result will be a composition where the parts work together with the whole to create a harmonious environment that is both historic, refined, sustainable and modest at the same time." To this Barbara adds that the facility also plans to provide a nurturing environment for American servicemen and servicewomen who are returning from wars with significant physical and mental disabilities. "As a workplace that holds out a hand to help others, stability and beauty will merge with nature," states Barbara. A challenging mission statement, but like the windswept Eastern Shore, clearly bolstered by solid muscle just beneath the surface.

warming wood

"It is the play of soft raking grey light on the coastal landscapes," muses Philip, "where aging and peeling painted wood boathouses nestle against pine and birch forests and granite shorelines. These are the images that are the most vivid for me when thinking of Sweden and the Baltic Sea."

FACING: Barbara takes a Swedish minimalist approach to the main house's entranceway, allowing the lines of the curved stairway and the various wood patinas to be the focal point. The Swedish bench bed is painted in traditional Falun red paint with blue detailing. Originally the day bed would pull out to make a bed for a child or servant but in contemporary times makes a fantastic, large storage bench.

BELOW: The stair and an early allmoge (or folk) Swedish bench display the simple beauty of paint and patina.

LEFT: A Swedish transitional mirror from 1760 hangs in the corner of the living room. Both the oil painting and the large pastel over the mantel are by Maryland artist Ruth Starr Rose. Chippendale camelback sofas are covered with sepia-colored quilted velvet. The large leather ottoman was designed by Barbara as a practical leather-covered boot rest after muddy gardening—the perfect example of form meets function.

ABOVE: While being warm and comfortable there is nothing excessive about this room. "Anchored both by a respect for nature, I think the early American and Swedish furniture work well together," says Barbara. "I love the mixture of the Kaare Klint chairs as they are twentieth-century attempts at reinterpreting the earlier Chippendale style."

LEFT: A rare built-in bed cupboard from an eighteenth-century Swedish stuga was acquired by Barbara in New England and brought down to Maryland, where it was installed in one of the upstairs guest rooms. Built-in beds such as this one served as private spaces in country farm homes where one room living around a hearth was not uncommon. Warm, cozy and practical, the built-ins were almost always dual purpose with cupboards, secretaries and even clocks forming the outside part of the unit. They are also warm, cozy and practical as Barbara dresses her bed up with pink toile and Swiss bed linens.

ABOVE: Intricate geometric moldings are the hallmarks of this Swedish cupboard bed from the north of Sweden. Eleish van Breems, Ltd., was instrumental in sourcing and advising Barbara and Philip on the rare Swedish antiques in their collection.

BELOW: In the ultimate salvage story, Barbara and Philip were able to rescue these rails from a local colonial estate that had once belonged to her ancestors and have incorporated them throughout the house. Barbara's brother painstakingly stripped the native yellow pine wood with special lead abatement techniques and then gently whitewashed and preserved the wood with a matte finish. The railings were then waxed with a lot of good old-fashioned elbow grease.

use native material

ABOVE: The Gunnery is the hunting lodge of Barbara's brother. The collection of eighteenth- and nineteenth-century furniture here is masculine and solid for relaxation after a day in a goose blind, stalking deer, or out fishing in the Chesapeake. The pale celadon tile stove was designed and built on-site to heat the Gunnery. "The length is extra long so that the gentle healing heat would be long enough for my brother to comfortably stretch out on. As he is 6'6", the construction was no small task!"

FACING ABOVE: Etchings and sketches are by Charleston, South Carolina's famous twentieth-century artist Alfred H. Hutty.

RIGHT: Rare horticultural books such as William Gilpin's Observations of Highlands of Scotland are among Barbara's collection.

ABOVE: A surprising American connection to the history of botanical exploration is that five naturalists in Colonial Maryland had collected native Maryland plant specimens between 1697 and 1736. The plants had been gathered and brought by boat to London for the famous Swedish botanist Carl Linnaeus. Linnaeus studied these plants in preparation for his groundbreaking book on botanical nomenclature, *Species Plantarum* (1753).

FACING: The tradition of using local native materials from your land or salvaged from the surrounding countryside has always been common in Sweden where resources were historically scarce. At Preservation Green, Barbara and Philip make a mission of rescuing materials from the past and incorporating those elements into their projects. Here, four-inch-thick marble slabs salvaged from Independence Mall in downtown Philadelphia surround Tilghman's therapy pool in the garden.

LEFT: The workspace for Barbara and Philip's privately funded horticultural research center incorporates Scandinavian touches, such as a Swedish eighteenth-century dome-topped painted bridal trunk under a bank of windows.

ABOVE: Open shelving is ubiquitous in Swedish homes. Shelving with a collection of Limoges, black basalt, books and wooden prototypes for Barbara's horticultural experiments hang above the tile stove and warming bench for easy access.

BELOW: The Baroque Viennese stove is a central gathering point as well as source of radiant heating in the Preservation Green research center offices. A red-painted Swedish antique drop-leaf table in the meeting area is among the many Swedish antiques put to everyday purpose again by Barbara and Philip.

Nurturing the present through the past—this is what Preservation Green does in the research center. Disabled servicewomen and servicemen are hired to assist in many experiments that relate to perfecting green roof design and also attractive ways to incorporate the natural world into increasingly hard-edged technical interior environments. A life-size Turkish Emperor decorates the top of an early 1700s stove warming heart and body, and greeting all who enter this restorative space.

City and Shore

JILL AND DANIEL DIENST

Jill Dienst, proprietor of Dienst + Dotter Antikviteter NYC is not only a historian of fine decorative elements but also an advocate for Scandinavian form and design. Straddling urban and country in this story, Jill's mix of Swedish high country from the Baroque and Gustavian periods poetically blend with contemporary art and fine Scandinavian pieces from design masters such as Poul Kjaerholm (1929–1980) and Arne Jacobsen (1902–1971).

Their apartment in New York was really meant to be a transitional space while the Dienst family looked for the perfect space to call home. While on her journey, which was to take a few years, Jill decided to reinvent their current apartment into an ode to a Swedish manor home. The space itself was very linear. The challenge for Jill was how to accomplish a proper metamorphosis. Calling upon influences from the great manor homes in Sweden, Jill commissioned artisans to help her transform her space into an inspirational backdrop for collections of eighteenth-, nineteenth- and twentieth-century Scandinavian antiques as well as her extensive collection of mid-century and contemporary photography.

Now located in New York City, Dienst + Dotter Antikviteter, Jill's antique shop located in Downtown New York City, is a treasure trove of rare and exotic seventeenth-, eighteenth-, nineteenth- and twentieth-century Scandinavian antiques and decorative elements. With an extensive background in the decorative arts, Jill's approach to her work is that of historian and preservationist first, dealer second. "I have been blessed in my early formative years to be influenced by many historians, dealers, designers and architects," explains Jill, "all of whom had a common trait even though they had very different perspectives—a good eye; a good eye for picking an unusual form and for placement for living. Hervé Aaron, Jacques Grange, John Pawson—all very different forms of genius that each had—and continue to have—a lasting impression on my own collecting and living." Jill's passion is to share her acquired knowledge with her clients,

An eighteenth-century Swedish rococo tall case clock, a nineteenth-century Swedish Leksand armchair, and painting by a Dutch sixteenth-century master welcome you in the main entrance foyer of the Dienst apartment.

Live with special pieces
without fear of living
too "specially."

and to tell the continued story of the fine craftsmen who have made the decorative arts in Scandinavia so valid.

The country residence of the Dienst family is in the heart of Sag Harbor, a short bike ride from town and the beach. A livable showcase of fine Scandinavian furnishings spanning the eighteenth to the twentieth centuries, it is Jill's escape from city life. By all accounts the fourteen-room colonial with pool house and guest barn is a place to not only house her collection but enjoy it with family and friends. Here, Jill says she tries to "live with special pieces without fear of living too 'specially.' None of us should forget that a chair was made for sitting—be it a seventeenth-century country piece, an eighteenth-century Manor house piece or a mid-twentieth-century modern piece. I always go back to forms that are sculptural AND functional." Jill has more than succeeded in transforming the 1810 historic American colonial home into an elegant and welcoming European home worthy of the finest historic homes in Scandinavia.

"When I think of Swedish design, I think of the craftsmen—perhaps unknown out of the corridors of power and influence in Stockholm—who toiled out of passion to created beautiful, functional things. In many cases we may never know their names or personal stories but those mysteries are partially solved through the beauty of what they left behind for us to enjoy for generations to come."

LEFT: The beauty of Scandinavian living is the balance of layers, textures and materials. Painted, upholstered, polished and sleek surfaces compose a symphony that is visually soothing to the eye.

ABOVE RIGHT: Shown is a wonderful example of period Gustavian carvings, fluting and marguerite details.

BELOW RIGHT: A close-up of an eighteenth-century Norwegian rococo leg carving detail that is based on form from nature. The Rococo period in Sweden and Norway celebrated the passion and spirit of art and nature. This carving almost appears to resemble the scales of a serpent breathing actual life into the table itself.

graceful lines

An eighteenth-century Swedish rococo latticework writing table is the perfect platform for Jill's prized collection of Swedish and Danish craftsman pottery by artist Arne Bang and Berndt Friberg.

ABOVE: Jill pulls together an accessory collection ranging from pieces from the seventeenth century up to the twentieth century to complement her workspace.

FACING: This wonderful writing table embodies the soul of eighteenth-century Swedish rococo; romance, passion, lyrical movement and the celebration of the female form. There is a defined earthiness to the table that is enhanced by the mix of period rococo accessories and a Danish stoneware bowl from twentieth-century Sweden.

ABOVE: Chairs in this dining room show a wonderful example of period Gustavian carvings, fluting and marguerite details.

RIGHT: An eighteenth-century rococo armchair anchors the entrance to the dining room.

Purity of form; integrity of design Without fussy adornment . . .

ABOVE: An overhead view of the library in Sag Harbor where a leather Arne Jacobsen Egg Chair and ottoman sit comfortably with an eighteenth-century Gustavian table. A Poul Henningsen artichoke pendant light hangs overhead.

FACING: A pair of eighteenth-century Gustavian tabouret is mixed with a rare Frits Henningsen–designed rocking chair and Poul Kjaerholm coffee table. Notice the Poul Henningsen pendant light in the front entrance hallway.

Eighteenth-century Swedish rococo side chairs surround a contemporary, round dining table. A Swedish eighteenth-century baroque chandelier and an eighteenth-century rococo gilt wood wall clock from Stockholm contribute depth and grounding to the light-filled room.

reflect light

Shown is a view to the kitchen where a balanced harmony exists between exterior and interior.

ABOVE: Scandinavian glass; well-loved, patina, wooden cutting boards; pewter; and terra-cotta tie elements sourced from nature to support the Scandinavian balance of form and function in symmetry with the environment.

FACING: Fine examples of furnishings from the rococo period in Sweden are on display in the master bedroom. Sand-washed floors enhance the original paint surfaces and patinas of the rare antiques.

ABOVE: Neutrals, linens and soft velvet set the tone for the room of Jill's daughter Emma, an experienced equestrian. The room boasts ribbons won as well as decorative elements ranging from fine oils to a pair of antique Swedish Dala (Dala Hest) horses from Dalarna, Sweden.

. . . Connection with Nature; perhaps a great metaphor for how we should live in these new times!

City and Shore | 121

ABOVE: The angular architectural detail of the picket fence contributes contrast to the linear boxwood hedge in front of the Dienst house in Sag Harbor.

FACING: The house was transported to the current location by ferry in 1810 and served as a meeting house in the town.

Romance on Duck Pond

SUSAN AND LARRY KESSLER

Homeowners Susan and Larry Kessler spent several years looking for the perfect property to build their home in Litchfield County, Connecticut. "We were looking for the house while we were living in London. Our brief to the estate agent was to find us a "romantic" property with water. After all, I am a Pisces," Susan says. While viewing the former estate of a well-known bandleader/composer and his wife, the Kesslers found their dream take root among the busy young birches and massive great oaks overlooking a substantial duck pond. Building was not going to be easy here, despite the bucolic setting. The original house would need to be torn down, and the new structure built in its place.

Inspired by an article about David Easton's country home in the New York Times in the early 1980s, which the Kesslers had saved, the couple knew they wanted to design a country home where they could relax in the country as well as entertain. Their motto was "small is the new big." After many months of research, Susan partnered with Connecticut-based Halper Owens Architects, a firm sensitive to historic properties. The journey began in earnest as principal architect Reese Owens helped Susan and Larry realize a plan for the construction.

According to Susan, "The order of the day for our project was to make the house as light and airy as possible with a minimal amount of furniture. The look is sophisticated and elegant but not too elegant for a country house. The palate is calming and the finishes key to making the house look old immediately. Many things were found in England, where Larry and I were living at the time. Attention to detail is fun for me even when building the house from far away. I am neurotic about detail. I also don't shy away from doing customized work once I find something that I like but isn't quite right."

Now that the structure was underway, Susan searched for a design team that would mesh seamlessly with her eye. "Given that this interior reflected the essence of Scandinavian interiors, the choice of Rhonda, Edie and their team at Eleish van Breems was a natural one. Nationally respected Scandinavian antiques dealers, designers, and bestselling

The elegance in Scandinavian form stems from the ability to create a functional form, yet the form itself is lyrical and one forgets that it is truly for a purpose.

authors of Swedish design books, they really had the background I was looking for. I liked their ability to communicate with me on many different levels to achieve the desired result." Attracted to European flavors and elegance, we saw that Susan wanted Duck Pond to be a home that was understated, refined, and yet a welcoming haven nestled harmoniously between the property's great wooded granite ridge and the fern-rimmed pond below. Feeling a kindred spirit and excited by the architectural plans, we were honored to take on the project.

At the time, the Kesslers were living in London (Susan, the co-editor of the Zagat London Restaurants Survey and Larry, a managing director at an international asset management firm), and a furious trans-Atlantic exchange, relying on e-mails, photos and many phone calls, ensued. Susan commuted periodically to the building site to work with Halper Owens Architects as well as our design team at Eleish van Breems. With an assembled team at hand on-site, and with Susan's direction from London as well as efficient visits, the mission to create Susan's vision of an inviting home with Swedish sensibility and in concert with the splendid property that surrounds the house, was accomplished.

BELOW: The stone gates to Duck Pond are flanked by antique copper lanterns that were restored by the Kesslers, and were original to the property.

FACING: The front entrance is parallel to the great room and runs from end to end.

let the light in

FACING: The Kesslers were preoccupied with wanting to have enough light in the house as to emulate architecture in Sweden. The cupola in the great room, the dormers in the porches and the triangle window fourteen feet off the ground in the kitchen ensure there is no lack of light.

LEFT: A cupola is the architecture focal point of the Kessler home.

FACING: Custom, Gustavian-inspired, built-in cabinetry, symmetrical to the room, were faux finished by Halperden Designs to create textured, layered depth to the room.

ABOVE: Exceptional carving detail on the front of this settee is rare and is the work of cabinetmakers, trained by the court of Gustav III, in eighteenth-century Stockholm.

RIGHT: A fine example of period Gustavian detailing and original paint surface can be seen on the apron of the Kesslers' great room occasional table.

ABOVE: Swedish eighteenth-century Pewter candlesticks and charger sit beautifully on the eighteenth-century French mantel.

RIGHT: As the Kesslers' main goal was to make the "new" house look "old," they purchased the eighteenth-century French fireplace mantel in London before construction had even begun.

The Kesslers' wrought iron kitchen table was customized based on a design for a side table, and the kitchen chairs were customized based on a design of high-backed barstools. The two cabinets flanking the entrance to the great room were created for the space based on antique Gustavian glass-front armoires. Faux finishing was applied to create multidimensional layers of color inspired by the historic colors from the northern region of Dalarna.

tone on tone

BELOW: The Kesslers commissioned custom handcrafted knobs and escutcheons.

FACING: The beauty of texture adds depth and elegance to a Gustavian-inspired interior. Multilayered faux-finished cabinets, lime-waxed antique flooring and fine chenille and fine embroidered textiles provide a subtle, tonal story.

LEFT: Egret paintings were commissioned so the birds were flying off in the direction of the pond. The love seats were custom designed based on ones the Kesslers saw in France.

ABOVE: Designed for the space, this custom chandelier provides essential light without fighting with other architectural elements in the room. To create a balance of space and a continuity of lines, a liming wash was applied to the antique, hand-hewn barn beams detailing the kitchen ceiling. Liming provided a softer, more authentic visual that complemented the antiqued, lime-wax flooring throughout the house.

BELOW LEFT: A view of lime-waxed antique flooring. Notice how the depth in wood grain is established by applying liming wax to natural, unfinished wood.

BELOW RIGHT: In keeping with the great manor homes of Scandinavia, careful detail was placed, as a finishing touch, in creating an organza wrap to cover the chain of the chandelier.

add a pinch
... of folk art

ABOVE: Scandinavian-inspired cut out motifs and lime-waxed railing complete the Kesslers' back stairwell.

RIGHT: At the top of the landing to the guest bedroom sits a rare eighteenth-century Swedish side chair, berry washer and water bucket from Dalarna (notice the unusual circular detail of the back).

LEFT: In keeping with the design of the house, the Gustavian-style bedroom is both a mix of custom-built pieces as well as antique finds. Toile-covered walls create a "jewel box" quality to the space.

ABOVE: A rare eighteenth-century Swedish Bonnard is displayed in the guest bedroom.

LEFT: As with most pieces in the master bedroom, with the exception of the eighteenth-century period Gustavian settee, this Gustavian commode was not only designed to look like an authentic Gustavian antique, but also serves an alternative purpose. Hidden and built within the piece is a flat-screen TV that rises with the help of a hydraulic mechanism. The photographs by Marcia Lippman were specifically placed to show off properly whether the TV was "up" or "down."

BELOW: Purchased and shipped from London for Duck Pond, the antique French crystal chandelier, ca. 1940, is the perfect complement to the Gustavian-style master bedroom. Similar to its Swedish counterpart, the French light fixture is airy, delicate and abundant with crystals to reflect light.

RIGHT: Located off one of the two porches, the space invites the natural surrounds of the exterior in. Sunlight is abundant and natural references are found in the wall and bed coverings as well as the sepia-toned collection of photographs by photographer Marcia Lippman.

Gustavian form is defined by a layer of functional pieces. Notice the delicate addition of the hand-blown glass lamp, providing a function, but yet not creating heaviness by barely being there.

Romance on Duck Pond | 145

FACING: Landscape designer Nancy McCabe created this enchanted bridge.

ABOVE: After researching many different types of outdoor furniture, Susan finally decided to go with the ones that she had her heart set on, even though it took forever and they came from Provence. As she said, "They make me smile."

The other key part of the team was Nancy McCabe who was responsible for the landscape design and stone work. These gigantic, antique slabs of bluestone had to be set in place before the house was completed given there wouldn't have been a way to get them in place on the site otherwise.

LEFT: A custom Munder-Skiles teak table is flanked by wrought iron side chairs from Hervé Baume in Provence. One of two porches on either side of the house, the summer dining terrace is screened in order to enjoy al fresco dining in the summer with an exquisite view of the trout pond below.

Oceanside Serenity

PATRICIA AND JEFFERY FISHER

Ask any artist and they will tell you that East Hampton, once the realm of fishermen and farmers, has a special light. They say it shimmers, it dances and that East Hampton is not a place but a state of mind illuminated by the reflection of two bodies of water flanking the South Fork of Long Island. Transformed from a farmers' community in the early twentieth century by wealthy families, artists and writers all looking for refuge from New York's oppressive summer heat, East Hampton remains one of the world's most sought-after communities. The combination of light, beaches and a vibrant arts community is appreciated by Patricia and Jeffery Fisher at their home in the Pudding Hill section of the village.

Purchased by Jeffery prior to their marriage, the 1920s cottage came to become a true reflection of Patricia and Jeffery's partnership as they lovingly restored the home together and put on an addition. Both took an active role in the project; Jeffery, by acting as general contractor, living on-site during construction, and Patricia, by designing the space and interior while commuting weekly from the city. Originally a head gardener or estate manager's house to a neighboring estate, the building had good bones but needed to be updated and expanded. A narrow main staircase was removed to enlarge the living room and a new airy foyer with staircase was added, pushing out the front of the house. A kitchen, guest room, library and sitting room were all added on with plenty of French doorways to maximize access to the Fisher's pool and extensive gardens.

Once construction and architectural detailing was completed, Patricia, principal of Patricia Fisher Design, started on the interior space. A fan of Swedish interiors, Patricia chose to incorporate Scandinavian "timeless design, clean lines, the element of surprise and of course comfort" to the house. Her love of Swedish painted furniture and its graceful purity

"I love Swedish painted furniture," declares Patricia. "It works beautifully with both modern and traditional settings. I am drawn to the blue grey tones and the painted surfaces that look particularly elegant when mixed with the creamy palette and blue accents I used throughout the house."

> "When I think of Swedish design, I think of beautifully made classic, functional furniture painted in serene greige tones."

worked seamlessly towards her goal to create a soothing and inviting place to relax and entertain. She is attracted to what she refers to as "the tranquil greige tones" of Swedish furniture. Derived from Sweden's love of all things French during the eighteenth century and especially associated with the classical Gustavian era, the white and grey palette was an inexpensive way for those unable to afford the gilt and rare wood furniture of the nobility, to at least copy what was so popular on the continent. The Gustavian style was simple, elegant and easy to replicate, and historically met with and was distilled into the roots of Swedish tradition when it traveled from the cities into the Swedish countryside, where it is referred to as "high country." Patricia finds this look works perfectly in her home as well as that of her clients.

Swedish antique pieces, such as a nineteenth-century blue tall case clock are mixed with sturdy Swedish reproductions from Chelsea Textile in some of the rooms. For larger spaces, such as the bedroom, where finding large Swedish furniture was problematic, Patricia designed custom pieces, including a bed and wall-length cupboard. Her use of solid as well as pale-grey-and-white-checked linens throughout the home and the pale greys, blues and taupe of the painted furniture create a mood that is soft and quite sumptuous without being imposing. Artwork in the form of sculpture, paintings and found architectural objects is prominently displayed. What makes Scandinavian interiors so refreshing and balanced is the inclusion of contemporary art mixed in with prized, heirloom antiques. The confidence to mix is natural and accepted. According to Patricia, this aesthetic comes as second nature to her, "I was an art dealer for many years. Being exposed to museum-quality fine art every day influenced me tremendously. I am always exploring and navigating the intersection of art and design." When asked what is her favorite part of Swedish design, she does not hesitate to say, "I love it all! The shapes and colors. Glorious, curvy clocks, everyday colors made to look rich, composed and timeless, and the uncluttered look of a well-edited room, the beautiful painted finishes. In the end, it really does have a sense of light most suitable to this part of the world."

Part of the 2007 renovation included the transformation of the main entrance staircase. Originally, the house lacked a foyer and the stairs were located in the living room. During the renovation, Patricia removed the existing staircase and created what is now a welcoming and airy two-level foyer with a new stairway.

ABOVE: The cottage on "Pudding Hill" is, according to Patricia, "a turn of the century shingled cottage located in the heart of the East Hampton historic district, two streets from the ocean." The interior was inspired by "late Gustavian-inspired furniture with classical design elements coupled with beautiful painted finishes, resulting in "a restrained and eclectic style with a sense of light."

RIGHT: Antiqued, natural French oak flooring, tonal and textural fabrics, simple window treatments, a classic Swedish tall case clock and horse, neutral walls and warm wood tones all help to establish a very inviting, Swedish-inspired, living room.

FACING: Provençal dining chairs and table add warm hues and grounding to the tonal, Swedish pigments of the walls and mirrors as well as the rug.

ABOVE: A mixing of worlds and styles: Traditional American Federal mirrors are painted with a Swedish finish as interpreted by Patricia.

BELOW: A nineteenth-century Scandinavian carving hangs opposite to the pair of Federal mirrors in the dining room. The whitewashed carving "pops" against the darker grey tones of the wall.

patina is poetry

a soft palette

ABOVE: Sitting on a nineteenth-century Gustavian-style console is a sculpture by an unknown artist. Notice how the round form of the ram complements the linear lines of the console.

RIGHT: The Gustavian sitting room is a beautiful pause point in the house. Glass French doors open to the outside and play off the eight-over-eight paned double windows on the opposite wall. Light streams into the room through the overhead skylights, doors and windows. Bold homespun checks play off the geometric patterned rug.

ABOVE: A view of the stairwell to the guest wing is where tonal mixes of pattern and texture create an inviting space within a space.

RIGHT: The kitchen, completely renovated with an addition added to make room for entertaining, reflects the key elements throughout the house. Natural, wide-planked French oak flooring and the Provençal farm table and chairs ground the otherwise clean, light-colored walls and dark counters. Stainless steel is introduced to add a reflective quality, and blue-and-white textiles are used to establish texture.

LEFT AND ABOVE: Traditional Swedish blues, whites and greys lend soothing hues to the master bedroom. Simple sheer blinds allow for the flow of light while adding a finished touch to the room.

BELOW: The Swedish crown is an important motif in Swedish design and décor. With a Gustavian-style armoire as a backdrop, this bed finial is one the many small, subtle details that are hallmark to Patricia's layered designs.

In the height of the summer, blooming, mature hydrangea and established gardens surround the porch and pool.

A Nordic Air

INGRID LEESS

Ingrid Bjelland Leess and her husband, Mark Larmee, live in a renovated 1940s farmhouse surrounded by woodlands and horse fields in southern Connecticut. Ingrid is an in-demand stylist, for over twenty-five years producing makeover and redesign stories for various national publications as well taking on private interior projects. Known for her Scandinavian color palette and textures, Ingrid's home is a wonderful example of how a traditional American farmhouse wholly lends itself to a Scandinavian-inspired interior.

Major influences of style came from Ingrid's parents, who were Swedish and Norwegian, and her appreciation for classic Scandinavian modern and antique design was nurtured at an early age. As Ingrid remembers, "Their home, when I was young, was entirely filled with Swedish and Danish modern furnishings. On trips back to Sweden, my Mother always brought back antiques from her childhood home. Other finds came from auctions, which I used to accompany her to. Swedish antiques . . . they are typically cleaner and closer to nature. You can see the human hand but still see the source from the northern woods."

In the light-filled rooms, Ingrid ties in all the subtle and key Scandinavian design elements. The whitewashed floors are effortlessly balanced by the placement of very simple Swedish rag rugs. Hand-blown glass and white pottery are prominently displayed in collections throughout the house as well as standing alone; on tables can be seen oversized centerpiece glass jugs and bubble glass sculpture. Natural straw is present in the form of woven lamps and ottoman, while sheepskin throws are naturally placed as seat coverings. A traditional trestle table is front and center in the living room. Marimekko fabric adds a final, contemporary pattern elevating these rooms from farmhouse to very chic interiors.

The sleek blue and white tiles and cabinetry in Ingrid's kitchen are softened by the addition of natural wood cutting boards and containers displaying plums, herbs and cut fig branches from the garden.

"I always start with as much natural

light as possible."

Elements of natural wood are peppered throughout the space, as well as many found objects. Above the fireplace is a dramatic art piece made from brown shipping paper and cardboard, and on the facing white wall is a large crushed metal box sculpture with rich brown rusted patina. Ingrid's artistic sensibility embraces the notion that fine art is everywhere if we can just learn to be still and look. "My last trip to Sweden, I spent most of my time in Göteborg, and my main mode for transportation was a bicycle. What a wonderful way to travel. You notice so much more when you slow things down."

LEFT: Simple, crisp white is grounded by natural tones. Elements of natural wood are peppered throughout the space, as well as the texture of woven straw and a very subtle and tonal Swedish rag rug. Pattern is introduced in the form of a single pillow.

ABOVE: Sitting still by the window is a concert of vessels derived from the earth: wood, clay, glass and a living plant.

A nineteenth-century pine Swedish measuring box gets a second life as a home for the rosemary topiary in the kitchen. These boxes were certified by the Swedish government yearly to confirm that the units were accurate for measuring. As a result, most measuring boxes have multiple stamps and markings.

"When I think of Sweden, I dream of eating cherries pulled from the tree in my Mor Mor's garden, eating mounds of crayfish with dill on those long summer days. Words . . . fresh and simple and delicious!"

FACING: The contemporary-inspired Leksand-style Swedish dining chairs flank the dining room's trestle table. Elements of Scandinavian inspirations are evident from the natural flooring, white-painted walls and alcoves and hand-blown glass accessories to the simple window treatments and abundant light.

BELOW: "I love how practical everything is in Sweden. Everything is so clean and smart . . . The design is so understated and comfortable . . . child friendly."

room to breathe

Scandinavian form and function is very apparent when looking at the built-in window seat. Rather than just a window seat, Ingrid designed the built-in seating with storage space below, thus creating a practical use as well as a functional one.

According to Ingrid, "I always start with bringing in as much outside light as possible, painting walls white and then layering in textures from nature."

LEFT: Hand-blown glass is introduced as an oversized centerpiece glass jug and accompanying bubble glass sculpture. Marimekko fabric finishes the space, adding that final, contemporary pattern elevating the room to a very chic interior.

ABOVE: A found wire object adds a sculptural, textured addition to the living room. This is a true example of the beauty of reclaimed materials as art.

In keeping with Ingrid's Scandinavian interiors, shades of blues, whites and neutral tones lend a perfect backdrop to the elegant home she has designed. Use of antique ticking, stripes and checks create texture to the tonal interior. All of the striped rope shades throughout the house were designed by Ingrid.

ABOVE: Due to the long, harsh winters, Scandinavian design has always incorporated the need for capturing the maximum amount of light possible in interiors. As a result, window treatments are simple and unconstructed to allow for the maximum amount of light.

BELOW: A pair of American nineteenth-century sandwich glass goblets is a seamless addition to the Scandinavian-inspired interiors. Again, key elements from nature (glass, wood, clay and a living plant) are on display reflecting the theme throughout the house. Nature is in harmony with the interior space.

ABOVE: Time rewards the collector. Ingrid has patiently bought and curated a fine collection of mostly Scandinavian pottery.

FACING: Ingrid's sitting room brings together Scandinavian design elements; bountiful light, simple window treatments, hand-blown glass, painted pine, natural flooring and living nature.

Nordic Soul

PAULA BATALI AND MICK AARESTRUP OF LIEF

Leaving the opaque morning haze of Los Angles, we pursue the sun as it rises and drive ourselves high up into the Hollywood Hills, where on a sunny hilltop dry plantings of salvias, lavender and aloes impart the lush cool feeling of a shade garden. Here, behind a tall stuccoed wall, Mick Aarestrup greets us at the private escape he and his wife designer Paula Batali have created at their 1930s hideaway house. The Mediterranean-style building appears at first to be all white-painted glamour with deep aquamarine blue trim. Mick throws open the doors to let us in and we are embraced by rooms where painted antiques of simple lines, natural materials and fine art all combine into a soothing space of deep personal expression.

Similar to their home, Mick and Paula seem to be the perfect exciting fusion of South American sophistication meeting Nordic soul. The couple's shared passion and ease with art and design reveals itself in their confident mix of decor. Elements, as disparate as a 1720s leather upholstered chair and an Anne Foresman painting, when put together in the intimate, domestic scale of the bungalow are totally energized. "It is best," says Mick, "to have a mixture of pieces, not all the same period. Just like we're all different from one another so are the homes we embody and the objects we fill them with. Everybody demands a certain amount of space, and plays very well with some and not so well with others. By mixing periods then, every piece gets their own voice." Both Swedish and South American designers seem to have mastered the power of mingling past and present as a very powerful means to evoke not just great beauty but also associations and sentiment.

> "At times it feels as though they literally have a soul."

Paula concurs that there is more similarity between Brazilian and Swedish design than one would initially suspect. "I am from Rio de Janeiro and consider myself very fortunate to come from a place where creativity and the design process is spontaneous, naïve and very much inspired by nature and materials. I believe that in this aspect, both countries have a similar approach to design. Brazilian furniture and interiors have a fluidity and an airy quality to them, and because of that, I was able to immediately relate to Swedish design."

In terms of living with antiques in modern settings, this is something she is entirely used to from her upbringing. A happy memory for Paula is of her father collecting antiques. "My family always seemed perplexed with my father's obsession—collecting really old and odd-looking stuff! Brazil is a new country! The antiques I was exposed to were mainly Portuguese Baroque; it was everywhere around my parents' apartment.

LEFT: The clean lines of an eighteenth-century Swedish drop-leaf table surrounded by Baroque period chairs look thoroughly modern when placed on a sisal rug in the uncluttered dining room. A tribal Northwest Indian mask hangs over the kitchen doorway. A painting dated 1917 by Russian artist Ragnar Ungern lends a bold focal point to the room, the painting's blues and blacks mirrored in the Swedish empire chandelier and Swedish eighteenth-century candlesticks.

ABOVE: The Swedish "slagbord" or drop-leaf table is famous among those familiar with Scandinavian furniture for its versatility and good looks. Folding down to often under a foot in width, the table may be pulled out and extended to make a work desk or table. Mick and Paula's eighteenth-century slagbord is painted in a whimsical faux blue marble.

Nordic Soul | 183

stack it

As for my mother, she was obsessed with concrete built-in furniture! So, I consider my father the 'antique dealer' and my mother the modernist. If you put all that together . . . here I am."

Mick's family, the Aarestrups, has been stylish suppliers for the Hollywood architectural and design elite for decades, starting with their father's arrival in California in the 1980s. Filling a void, Aarestrup's gallery, Lief, quickly became a mainstay for those looking for interesting Scandinavian design. "We were so fortunate growing up in Sweden to have parents and grandparents that were collectors, in a beautiful, passionate home, built in 1628, where artists would come and go. I am building upon a foundation that is deeply rooted," says Mick appreciatively. With art and antiques in his soul and upbringing, Mick went on to study Art at RISD while his brother Stefan took a business approach and degree. Both brothers now run Lief and together make a formidable team.

The store, located in the Almont design district, is an elegant, airy space housed in a 15,000-square-foot warehouse that used to be an industrial dye shop. At Lief there is to be found a mix of many periods of Scandinavian design from the Baroque and Gustavian to modern masters such as Finn Juhl, Asplund, and Kaare Klint mixed in with contemporary artists for good measure. All of the furniture, carefully selected by Mick and Stefan, has a distinct blend of simple lines and opulent natural materials.

Mick walks us through the Lief showrooms with Paula and shares that "What I love most about Swedish eighteenth-century design is the beauty of its imperfections. The off-kilter chair and the worn patina is part of what gives each piece its soulfulness." Paula agrees as she points out a rare Gustavian court table, "Swedish design is more toned down compared to French and Italian, and yet extremely elegant and classic—its form beautiful and harmonious. The pieces evoke such warmth that at times it feels as though they literally have a soul. I also find fascinating how the designer/design always has function in mind, as opposed to just being a decorative object. I think that the concept of less-is-more definitely works in this case." In what could describe the couple's overall design philosophy, Mick concludes, "Swedish design has a refined, yet extremely sophisticated humbleness. These are things we return to again and again in our own home and for our clients—authenticity, soulfulness, humor."

In keeping with Swedish functionality and practicality, everyday objects such as dishes are stacked and left in full view. Here, the dishes and glasses are stored in a glass-front Baroque Swedish cabinet, their simple beauty standing proud next to a metal sculpture by contemporary Finnish artist Merja Winqvist.

Mick and Paula create a three-way conversation across centuries by placing their Baroque embossed leather chair next to art by contemporary French artist Anne Delfieu and hanging a 1940s Lyfa light pendant above.

When I think of Sweden . . .
a magical light,

naiveté, nature, fairytale...

fantastic design... and an extremely civilized nation!

"Design should be, and is for me, completely personal."

THIS PAGE: This Baroque stool in embossed leather and worn red patina is from a castle in the south of Sweden. Its companion, a matching chair from the same castle, shares the room and is followed in color by the Baroque glass cupboard and an art piece by Anne Delfieu.

FACING: A seventeenth-century Swedish bowl in alder root with ivory cabochons.

every object holds a secret

Nordic Soul | 193

Cooks who enjoy entertaining quite a bit, Mick and Paula renovated their kitchen to be utilitarian, functional, and easy to clean and organize. The industrial feel of the sleek steel makes a wonderful contrast to the antiques and overall look of the house. Warm touches such as the rag rug and antique wooden bowls ground the space and make it inviting. Traditional Swedish open shelving hangs throughout the small kitchen and a commercial storage unit with glass doors keeps pantry items and plates in view.

LEFT: French 1930s club chairs nestle by the fireside and are watched over by a nineteenth-century Buddha. The blue trunk is from Dalarna, Sweden, an area known for its rich folk art.

ABOVE: Mick and Paula love to spend time outside on the terrace. "Reading, dining, entertaining, swimming or just staring at the incredible nature around us! It's such a fantastic place," says Paula. "We're surrounded by wildlife. Deer walk on the hill right across from the house, hawks and ravens fly over the tall canopy of trees, and owls sing at night."

BELOW: As a nod to Sweden, birch trees have been planted in the courtyard around the pool, evoking the Northern forests of a John Bauer. "In my dreams I'm being carried away by Bauer's giant elk from the story Lilla Carla! His illustrations are exceptionally pure and poetic. It literally takes me to another world," says Paula.

A pair of Gustavian chairs by Melchior Lundberg flank a Russian Empire birch secretary.

LEFT: Lief is an inviting treasure trove of Scandinavian antiques with a massive hanging dried foliage installation by Paula acting as a focal point in the large space. The colored glass lamps are by Carl Fagerlund.

ABOVE: These simple Swedish eighteenth-century bowls, hand carved from birch and pine, are art in themselves as beautifully displayed by Mick and Stefan at Lief.

BELOW: A painted Italian plinth opens up for storage inside.

ABOVE: "Folk art doesn't get much credit. I believe that most people let the poetry of the pieces or designs escape from their eyes—for many different reasons."

FACING: Swedish painted furniture of the eighteenth century, as seen here in a rococo clock, cabinet and chair, has a soft chalk-like appearance derived from the native mineral pigments used in the paint. Combine the soft glow of the original paint color with a worn patina and you have something amounting to perfection.

One of Mick and Stefan's rarer pieces at Lief is this table form Gustav III's Royal Cabinet. "Whenever you find a period Gustavian piece in its original gold, it is almost always a royal piece," says Mick. "During the late nineteenth and early twentieth centuries, a lot of Swedish pieces were gilded but the finish on those pieces is much more flat than what you see on this eighteenth-century table."

California Calm

LINDA AND LINDSAY KENNEDY

Linda Kennedy's style is highly influenced not only by Sweden but by the taking leave of it at a young age to pursue the pleasures of the sun and beaches of California—mix this in with a love of Belgian aesthetic and you have the foundations of Linda's distinctive interior design work. "I love things to be simple even when using bright punctuations of color," says Linda, "and I especially need calm and simplicity in my interiors." Nestled among olive trees and hedges of orange and hornbeam, the Kennedy's house rises up into the side of a hill, where the feeling of ascent is accentuated by narrow steps flanked by suspending ornaments of climbing ivy and hydrangea. Once up in her aerie, interior designer Linda prefers the carefree modernity of a cool white-and-grey palette offset by the green of the garden and verdant views of the surrounding Hollywood Hills. An avid collector and former antiques dealer, Linda employs lots of Swedish antiques into her home, each edited and carefully considered for their line and form, as well as for their sleek, softly painted patinas. The atmosphere is cool and fresh, a place of sanctuary and family for Linda, her husband, restaurateur Lindsay, and their son, Christopher.

"When Lindsay and I found this house it was all dark wood and dark paint colors but I loved the space, and the living room I imagined completey white when I saw it. The size is comfortable for us right now, with an upper floor, backyard garden built into the hill, and lots of windows and light." The large living room has a soaring, vaulted, white ceiling that is grounded by iron tie beams. The couple limed and oiled the floorboards a Swedish, traditional, light-enhancing flooring style. The centerpiece of the living room is a clock cupboard featured in their previous home that Linda thinks of now as a signature piece. "Every day, I get more contemporary in my approach to this home and the antiques have become really my art pieces." Comfortable linen-covered sofas and armchairs are made glamorous by sleek modern drink tables and a large charcoal work on paper of a dancer glides across one of the walls. A step up from the fireplace is the dining

The mellow patina of an eighteenth-century Swedish chair and rare clock secretary act as artwork when offset by the white walls of the living room.

form loves function

ABOVE: The hand-carved curvilinear details of the clock case have a grace of form that is echoed in the pewter plates displayed on the top of the clock secretary.

LEFT: A transformation in white. Linda and Lindsay replaced the dark cherry floors and dark-painted walls to a lighter palette after purchasing their Laurel Canyon bungalow.

The iron tie beams are decorative and original to the house. Linda decided to leave them installed to ground the all-white living room.

area, where a Swedish nineteenth-century trestle table is offset by six slick IKEA versions of Arne Jacobson chairs. A center door behind the table is the entrance to professional chef Lindsay's efficiently tricked-out industrial kitchen with an eight-range stove. Owner of the popular Village Idiot restaurant in Hollywood and the soon-to-open Black Cat in Silver Lake, Lindsay's focus on culinary arts and great entertaining for guests and family is the other heart and masterful eye at play in this home. Fresh herbs on the windowsill and Christopher's school papers and baseball gear is in evidence on a Swedish farm table that serves as a rugged desk and computer table. The garden is an intimate enclosure off the bedrooms. All is simple and serene.

Linda admits that her style has been evolving ever since becoming a lead designer, overseeing the interior design of exclusive properties monthly in Los Angeles, Florida, New York and Connecticut markets for Meridith Baer Home. "Meridith taught me the basics," says Linda, "and is someone who allows you to express yourself. She has opened my eyes wider. I am excited by the trade shows Meridith and I attend and seeing all the new pieces, where I always bring something special home. I love right now the lamps and acrylic square boxes with rope handles. These contemporary pieces always look great mixed with the older pieces."

"Aesthetically. The way I see things," says Linda when asked how Swedish design has influenced her. "Honestly, Swedish design helps me every day because it is a touch point I can return to—that basic simplicity. I just love coming home; I feel super peaceful in this very calm environment. After a crazy day I can return, take a deep breath and relax instantly. All is calm, the all-white neutrality also allows me to reset my mind and then move on to the next design thought."

> Swedish design helps me every day. It is a touch point I return to—the basic simplicity.

French doors open onto a small sunroom where a moss thrives in a rustic urn on a Swedish early-nineteenth-century drop-leaf table. A modern cane stool is finished with a casual pillow of Belgium linen. Traditional to Sweden and Belgium, linen is used as upholstery throughout the house.

lighten the floors

FACING: California sunlight takes on a Northern feeling, streaming through the front door onto the white-stained pine flooring.

LEFT: A charcoal of a dancer by the contemporary artist Brianna Smith hangs prominently in the living room. "Brianna Smith is a great artist. I needed art and she came over and taped some paper on the wall and just did it! The result is the dancer and flowers in the bedroom."

ABOVE: When it comes to flowers, Linda prefers simplicity, saying that "loose small arrangements of one type of flower, like these poppies, are my favorite."

FACING: A small oil landscape given to Linda by her mother that once belonged to her grandfather hangs next to a Gustavian cupboard in the hallway leading to the bedrooms.

ABOVE: A Gustavian chair shows a faded and worn patina.

not just white, many whites!

FACING: The antique Swedish pine trestle table with IKEA dining chairs is set on the landing leading into the kitchen. Wood piled next to the fireplace is visible by the landing.

RIGHT: Horn candlesticks and a large stoneware pot with sedum make a tablescape.

LEFT: The warmth of natural wood is brought out by contrast with the metal legs of the modern chairs.

"Everything is very calm. I take a deep breath and relax and reset my mind."

LEFT: The master bedroom leads out onto the back garden that is surrounded by orange and horn hedges. The bed's headboard is custom made of extra-thick Belgian linen.

ABOVE: A rustic eighteenth-century Swedish burl bowl with original red paint sits atop an eighteenth-century Swedish sideboard.

Inspired Voyage

TARA SHAW

A city of international commerce since its beginnings as a trading post on the Mississippi River, the unique culture and architecture of New Orleans has inspired writers, musicians and artisans for centuries. Even Bob Dylan has attempted to distill the city's essence and writes in his memoirs that,

"The city is one very long poem. Flower-bedecked shrines, white myrtles, bougainvillea and purple oleander stimulate your senses, make you feel cool and clear inside. Everything in New Orleans is a good idea. Bijou temple-type cottages and lyric cathedrals side by side. Houses and mansions, structures of wild grace. Italianate, Gothic, Romanesque, Greek Revival standing in a long line in the rain. Roman Catholic art. Sweeping front porches, turrets, cast-iron balconies, colonnades—30-foot columns, gloriously beautiful—double pitched roofs, all the architecture of the whole wide world and it doesn't move."

Among the contemporary contributors to New Orleans' ever-eclectic design mix is the interior designer and antiques dealer Tara Shaw. With imports arriving regularly from her prolific European antiques jaunts and her own popular Tara Shaw MAISON line manufactured in the Crescent City and also hand carved and painted in Asia, Tara has found her niche as one of the largest antiques and furniture dealers to the South and is busy expanding her company globally.

The exterior of Tara's château-style residence is dressed in French eighteenth-century restraint. Here nature is tamed and a verdant green lawn surrounded by hedges, topiaries, formal sculpture and parterres leads to a lacquered door reminiscent of black onyx. The formal façade quickly dissolves, however, when Tara and her husband, Robby Walsh, welcome us as their pair of white whippets frolic like lively children around their feet. In her relaxed kitchen, filled with Italian and Swedish antiques, Tara describes how she finds her home in the city's Uptown area to be an oasis from

An eighteenth-century Swedish tall case clock with a decorative neoclassical urn finial top overlooks a Swedish eighteenth-century drop-leaf table in the dining area of the kitchen. The Swedish-style chairs, from Tara's MAISON line are upholstered in practical dove grey leather from Holly Hunt.

her international business schedule as well as a private place to put her design theories to work. "My full schedule has always been the inspiration to the 'calming effect' of what I want clients to experience when they come home.

The relaxed feel of well-loved Swedish antiques with original worn patinas is visually soft and pleasing to the eye and they work effortlessly with contemporary furnishings and architecture. "Tara's love of creating a design for living that is based on layering the present over the past without compromising either one, is evident as she takes us through the house where Swedish furniture is used in each room. The house already had fine proportions and scale and was made to exacting standards by the previous owner. Under Tara's deft touch, simple but powerful forms from different centuries now play in the tall sunlit rooms side by side. Swedish modern chairs in the living room by Arne Norell, for example, offset a medieval gilt sculpture and Italian walnut veneer table. "I love Arne Norrell for his vision on a truly comfortable man-scaled chaise. His style is clean, elegant and timeless and most of all works so well with eighteenth- and nineteenth-century Swedish furniture and their classic streamline silhouettes."

Contemporary paintings and sculpture are mixed with antiquities and painted Swedish furniture. By contrasting the patina of time with sleek modern elements, a tension is created—each enhancing the other. "I basically have had a passion for painted furniture for over two decades and the love affair with painted Swedish, for me, is that one can visually see the texture because of the use of grainy woods under the painted surface. I love contrasting these painted pieces with sleek mid-century modern in my own home as well as those of my clients."

The upstairs takes us into a more romantic realm where the guest bedroom blends Empire restraint with Gustavian light and simplicity. Tara's photography of a sphinx is echoed in the inscrutable sphinx and griffins in the Gustavian mirror hung on a facing wall. "In design, a mirror will always open the space and reflect other items in the room," states Tara. "It really adds the third dimension and I always grade a room by the lighting—it is one of the first things I notice. All spaces need a unique anchor and so I say, 'Let there be light!'" A soft white leather hide rug on the wide-planked floor, creamy white draperies and bedding all give the room a further Nordic air and make a great contrast to the textured painted antiques and rich browns of the room's mahogany bed and leather chair.

Tara takes a cue from seventeenth- and eighteenth-century faux panels in her showroom located at the edge of the Garden District and Warehouse District on Camp Street in New Orleans. Wood paneling in Europe during the Baroque period and the Enlightenment was all the rage as both a practical and attractive way of insulating a room and hiding irregularities. At the height of the style, these boiseries were sumptuously carved, painted and designed by master decorative architects and artisans and it is a joy to report that examples of these remarkable rooms can still be found throughout many fine palaces and manor homes of Europe. In Sweden, elaborately carved wood paneling was very costly, reserved for the nobility, and so canvases painted in faux paneling were used instead.

The walls in Tara's showroom are painted in soft hues of white, sand and ochres depicting delicate paneling inspired by a library in Italy and referencing eighteenth-century Sweden. Two massive antique Italian bookcases with vellum volumes and mounted shells line the entry room where Tara's reproduction Swedish table and chairs from her Tara Shaw MAISON line invite clients to sit and browse her extensive catalog of 260 reproduction pieces.

Realizing that fine antiques were being exhausted from the market, Tara started her MAISON line of reproduction

Evoking the culinary air of the kitchen, a still life with fish by the nineteenth-century French artist Trouillebert hangs in the breakfast room. The table is set with French-style cloches from the Tara Shaw MAISON line. A delicate tassel hangs from the Époque Louis XIV chandelier in the kitchen dining area.

Contemporary, mid-century, seventeenth- and eighteenth-century art and furnishings all mingle and complement each other in the living room. A painting by Steven Seinberg floats above the grand piano and a pair of chairs by Swedish designer Arne Norell stand on either side of an Italian walnut inlaid round table.

furniture to supply a need for beautiful antique forms. Working closely with manufacturers and artisans in New Orleans, India and China, Tara's furniture line is known for its exacting attention to patina and detail. Reflecting on who in Swedish design and home furnishings she admires and would love to speak with, Tara states that "My conversation would be with Ingvar Kamprad, the founder of IKEA. Beauty begets beauty and I am of the opinion that beautiful furnishings are not just for the 1 percent. There is something universally significant about a man's home being his castle. Ingvar's worldwide vision of attainability of furniture and accessories that are made in price ranges for all to enjoy is to be admired." This is one of the key philosophies behind Tara sharing her extraordinary antiques collection as reproductions, to enable the rare forms to carry on and be enjoyed by all—proving, like most everything in New Orleans, to be a very good idea indeed.

LEFT: This eighteenth-century Swedish banquette is upholstered in mohair and has matching mohair bolsters with eighteenth-century metallic trim. The vintage Fortuny pillows are by Tara's friend Becky Vizard. Tara found the seventeenth-century statue in Isle sur la Sorgue, France. "I was told it was a representation of St. Elizabeth but I do not really know her true identity."

FACING: The Italian canapé in the limestone entrance hall is painted with diamonds to mimic inlaid marble. The eighteenth-century Empire Italian silverleaf chandelier makes a dramatic focal point, hanging from the double-story stairwell.

A painting by Louisiana artist Pellegrin hangs over a trunk from Torino, Italy, in the upstairs landing.

"I love the hand-cut crystal on the Swedish eighteenth-century candelabras."

LEFT: A white hide adds a Scandinavian flair to the landing along with a Gustavian period lyre-back chair and Swedish eighteenth-century rococo bench. Folding screens upholstered in English lacquered linen flank the dramatic urn in the windows of the landing.

ABOVE: The Italian wood urn and acrylic plinth are both part of the Tara Shaw MAISON collection.

Inspired Voyage | 233

linens

ABOVE: This fine French eighteenth-century table is one of the first antiques Tara ever bought.

BELOW: An Italian painted black and gilt corona lends a royal touch to the guest bedroom.

meet leather

Mixing Swedish eighteenth-century and French Empire creates a room that is both calming and elegant. The eighteenth-century Italian reclining chair from Cuneo, Italy, adds bold lines contrasting with the soft drapery, bed curtains and hide rug.

paint glorious paint

LEFT: The main showroom at Tara Shaw is painted in soft hues of ivory, sand and ochre. Swedish rococo armchairs flank a Swedish bench bed decorated with griffins.

ABOVE: Italian and French candelabras glisten on almost every surface in Tara's store.

FACING: The half-moons sometimes seen on late-eighteenth-century Swedish tall case clocks actually are symbols of the element salt and define the piece as having come from a mining town such as Sala, Sweden.

ABOVE: A Swedish tall case clock in Tara's showroom has hand-carved geometric detailing.

RIGHT: This eighteenth-century Italian armchair has the delicate lines shared by Swedish and French furniture of the period.

"beauty begets beauty"

ABOVE: Sprays of eucalyptus and peony blossoms in a French urn are just one of the many small touches that complete the romantic mood in the Tara Shaw showrooms.

RIGHT: A rare Swedish rococo bench, next to the Swedish extended dining table, was one of the fine antiques that inspired the Tara Shaw MAISON line.

A plethora of treasures awaits in the Tara Shaw showrooms.

"I am of the opinion that beautiful furnishings are not just for the 1 percent. There is something universally significant about a man's home being his castle."

"I always grade a room by the lighting—it is one of the first things I notice. All spaces need a unique anchor and so I say, 'Let there be light!'"

The Elements of Swedish Style

There are certain design elements that we see used continuously throughout Sweden and in all of the homes highlighted in these pages. Although many of these components are not unique to Sweden, when used in concert they impart the basic substance and attitude of Swedish style. We invite you to delve into these Elements and take the Swedish perspective—we think you will love the view.

SWING A CHANDELIER

Mirrors, gilt brass and crystal chandeliers have been used for centuries in Swedish design to capture the fleeting light of winter and to celebrate and reflect the long summer days.

FIND A BALANCE

From the proportions on a carefully designed piece of furniture to the relationship of negative to positive space in a room, Swedish design always strikes a balance.

RICH LEATHER

From sheepskin throws to rich leather upholstery, leather lends a sense of both luxuriousness and durability.

MIX OLD AND NEW

Swedish homes are highly personal and antique heirlooms are mixed side by side next to the most current designs, creating sophisticated design dynamics.

FLORA SUECIA

A tradition of floral motifs dating back to the great Swedish botanist Carl Linnaeus. Sweden's love affair with flowers can be found on furniture carvings to glass and textiles.

BOLD COLOR

Use of deep saturated colors in paints and textiles are historic to Sweden and are still used today to brighten and cheer the long dark winters.

BRING THE OUTDOORS IN

The relationship between Man and Nature is very revered in Sweden and there is always a bit of nature brought into the Swedish home.

USE THE UNEXPECTED

Swedish whimsy is just that; using materials in fun, new and unexpected ways.

WARMING WOOD

Wood and the forests represents the essence of life to Swedes and even just a stack of logs brought inside can lift the mood with its promise of warmth.

USE NATIVE MATERIALS

Historically, Sweden was geographically isolated from the continent, so featuring indigenous materials such as stone, iron or wood found locally is part of Swedish design tradition. Use local materials in your own home to deepen a sense of place.

GRACEFUL LINES

The restraint of decoration, functionality and perfection of lines is at the heart of Swedish design philosophy.

REFLECT LIGHT

Glass is revered as an art form in Sweden and lots of it is enjoyed in interiors for its beauty and reflective quality.

LET THE LIGHT IN

Window treatments are sparse in Swedish homes as light is a rare and highly valued commodity for most of the year.

TONE ON TONE

Base palettes in Sweden tend towards rich combinations of slightly different shades of one or two colors lending an overall soothing and calming effect.

ADD A PINCH OF FOLK ART

Swedish folk art, often handed down within families, is appreciated as an art form to be celebrated and easily mixes with contemporary pieces.

PATINA IS POETRY

The patina on Swedish antique furniture is beloved for its dry chalky finish derived from thin applied layers of mineral pigment paints.

ROOM TO BREATHE

Swedish interiors maintain a balance of positive to negative space. The key here is not a lot of clutter and broad areas of empty floor space.

A PLACE TO DREAM

A Swede knows that cozy, often romantic resting and reading areas are central to well- being and the imagination.

STACK IT

From hanging plate racks to open bookshelf units, Swedes like to keep everyday objects out in the open and accessible.

EVERY OBJECT HOLDS A SECRET

The home in Sweden is an extremely personal expression and acts as a mirror to the owner's travels, interests and passions. Design trends take a back seat to personal expression.

HANG ART

Art is a huge part of cultural life and is essential to the Swedish home, gracing nearly every room.

FORM LOVES FUNCTION

Practical furniture hybrids that serve double duty have their origins in Sweden's stuga country living, when life for the majority was often in close quarters. Beds with built-in clocks and cupboards, benches that convert into pull-out beds and chairs that can turn into tables are just a few of the many ingenious space-saving furniture forms found in Swedish design.

LIGHTEN THE FLOORS

Light floors reflect sunlight, a precious commodity in Sweden. Lime and Danish oil are the traditional ways to treat floorboards.

NOT JUST WHITE, MANY WHITES

Simplicity is never that simple—the "white palette" that is associated with Swedish design is almost always layers of whites, greys and soft mellowed natural wood surfaces mixed in with lots of texture to keep it all from being hard-edged.

GATHER THE WORLD TOGETHER

A Swedish home reflects the often far-flung and exotic travels of its owners and a global perspective is embraced.

LINENS MEET LEATHER

Prized for their durability and textures, linen and leather are two of the oldest materials used in upholstery and floor treatments in Sweden.

PAINT GLORIOUS PAINT

From the Falun red paints, derived from byproducts of Sweden's copper mines, to the mellow mineral pigments used by decorative painters, Sweden's love affair with painted furniture and wall surfaces continues to this day.

Resources

INTERIOR DESIGNERS AND ARCHITECTS

2Michaels Design
360 Central Park West, Suite 16H
New York, NY 10025
212.662.5358
www.2michaelsdesign.com

Barbara Paca and Philip Logan
Preservation Green
437 East 12th Street
New York, NY 10009
212.358.0538
preservationgreenllc.com

Eleish van Breems, Ltd.
P.O. Box 313
Washington Depot, CT 06794
860.354.0700
www.evbantiques.com
www.swedishinteriors.blogspot.com
www.deringhall.com/eleish-van-breems

FLANK
Architecture, Development, Brokerage
520 West 27th Street, Suite 403
New York, NY 10001
212.352.8224
www.flankonline.com

Patricia Fisher
Patricia Fisher Design
East Hampton, NY
917.324.0586
www.patriciafisher.com

Ann Ljungberg and Rajesh Kumar
Just Scandinavian
New York, NY
212.334.2556
www.justscandinavian.com

Laserow Antiques & Design
200 Lexington Avenue
New York, NY 10016
212.988.9194
www.laserowantiques.com

Paula Batali and Mick Aarestrup, Lief
642 North Almont Drive
West Hollywood, CA 90069
310.492.0033
www.liefalmont.com

Linda Kennedy
Meredith Baer Home
4820 Everett Court
Vernon, CA 90058
310.204.5353
www.meredithbaer.com

Halper Owens Architects
225 Mill Street
Greenwich, CT 06830
203.531.5341

18 Titus Road
Washington Depot, CT 06794
860.868.4000
www.halperowens.com

Ingrid Leess
Ingrid Leess Design
New Canaan, CT 06840
www.ingridleessdesign.blogspot.com

Nancy McCabe Garden Design
163 Dublin Road
Falls Village, CT 06031
860-824-0354

Tara Shaw
Tara Shaw Maison
1240 Camp Street
New Orleans, LA 70130
504.525.1130
www.tarashaw.com

Jonas Wickman
Arcanum Swedish Design
+46 (0) 707 72 84 01
www.arcanumswede.com

ARTISANS AND WORKROOMS

A & D Upholstery
Custom upholstery, drapery, pillows
Woodbury, CT
203.263.7277

Angel Threads
Custom drapery and pillows
718.462.0455
www.angelthreadsnyc.com

Don Lawson
Master Craftsman
203.770.1380

Eva Badenhorst

Muralist
Artist's Representative:
    Eleish van Breems, Ltd.
P.O. Box 313
Washington Depot, CT 06794
860.354.0700
www.evbantiques.com

Peter Germain

Custom drapery and upholstery
931 Bantam Road
Bantam, CT 06750
860.567.1442

Harpenden Design

Decorative paint finishes and murals
193 Simpaug Turnpike
West Redding, CT 06896
203.938.2613

Ives Brothers Painting, Inc.

44 Kasson Road
Bethlehem, CT 06751
203.266.5008
alan@ivesbrothers.com

Metal Works North

Metal restoration, refinishing and ironwork
203.723.9075

Munson Colonial Builders

Robert Munson Jr.
Box 252
Roxbury, CT 06783
860.354.1665
bob@munsoncolonialbuilders.com

Scofield Historic Lighting

90 Ivoryton, CT 06442
860.767.7032
www.scofieldhistoriclighting.com

Vitanza Furniture Finishers

Custom upholstery
718.401.1022
www.vitanzafurniture.com

ANTIQUES, FURNISHINGS AND ACCESSORIES

Ann Koerner Antiques

4021 Magazine Street
New Orleans, LA 70115
504.899.2664
annkoerner@annkoerner.com
www.annkoerner.com

A. Tyner Antiques

The Galleries of Peachtree Hills
425 Peachtree Hills Avenue
Building 2, Suite 13
Atlanta, GA 30305
404.367.4484
atynerant@gmail.com
www.swedishantiques.biz

B4

539 East 12th Street
New York, NY 10009
212.505.5344
info@b4decor.com
www.b4decor.com

Bjork Studio

1190 Old Chattahoochee Avenue, NW
Atlanta, GA 30318
404.350.8133
info@bjorkstudio.com
www.bjorkstudio.com

Brian Kish, Inc.

27 Greene Street
New York, NY 10013
212.925.7850
www.briankish.com

The Country Gallery Antiques LLC

P.O. Box 70
1566 Route 315
Rupert, VT 05768
802.394.7753
antiques@countrygallery.com
www.country-gallery.com

Country Swedish

22 Elizabeth Street
South Norwalk, CT 06854
203.855.1106
www.countryswedish.com

Cupboards & Roses Swedish Antiques

296 South Main Street, Route 7
Sheffield, MA 01257
413.229.3070
www.cupboardsandroses.com

Dawn Hill Antiques

11 Main Street
New Preston, CT 06777
860.868.0066
www.dawnhillantiques.com

Dienst + Dotter Antikviteter

411 Lafayette Street
New York, NY 10003
212.861.1200
www.dienstanddotter.com

Eileen Lane Antiques, Inc.

236 East 60th Street
New York, NY 101022
212.474.2988
www.eileenlaneantiques.com

Eleish van Breems, Ltd.
P.O. Box 313
Washington Depot, CT 06794
860.354.0700
www.evbantiques.com
www.swedishinteriors.blogspot.com
www.deringhall.com/eleish-van-breems

Ericson Gallery
P.O. Box 12212
Des Moines, IA 50312
515.279.0591
tom@ericsongallery.com
www.ericsongallery.com

Evergreen Antiques
200 Lexington Avenue, 10th Floor
New York, NY 10016
212.744.5664
www.evergreenantiques.com

H. M. Luther
The Carlyle
35 East 76 Street
New York, NY 10021
212.439.7919

Greenwich Village
61 East 11 Street
New York, NY 10003
212.505.1485
www.hmluther.com

Hostler Burrows
51 East 10th Street
New York, NY 10013
212.343.0471
www.hostlerburrows.com

Karl Kemp Antiques
Uptown
833 Madison Avenue
New York, NY 10021
212.288.3838

Downtown
34-36 East 10th Street
New York, NY 10003
212.254.1877
www.karlkempcom

Klaradal Swedish Antiques & Gifts
16644 Georgia Avenue
Olney, MD 20832
301.570.2557
www.klaradal.com

Just Scandinavian
New York, NY
212.334.2556
www.justscandinavian.com

Laserow Antiques & Design
200 Lexington Avenue
New York, NY 10016
212.988.9194
www.laserowantiques.com

Lars Bolander LTD.
3731 South Dixie Highway
West Palm Beach, FL 33405
561.832.2121

232 East 59th Street
New York, NY 10022
212.924.1000
www.larsbolander.com

lief
646 North Almont Drive
Los Angeles, CA 90069
310.492.0033
www.liefalmont.com

Lillian August
Lillian August Designs, Inc.
32 Knight Street
Norwalk, CT 06851
203.857.4336
www.lillianaugust.com

Lone Ranger Antiques
954.925.8990
www.lonerangerantiques.com

Masters & Pelavin
13 Jay Street
New York, NY 10013
646-926-2787
www.masterspelavin.com

R twentieth Century
R Gallery
82 Franklin Street
New York, NY 10013
212.343.7979
www.rtwentiethcentury.com

Ryder Antiques
905.639.4407
www.ryderantiques.com

Scandinavian Antiques and More
1760 S. Broadway
Denver, CO 80210
303.722.2541
www.scandinavianantiques.com

Scofield Historic Lighting
90 Ivoryton, CT 06442
860.767.7032
www.scofieldhistoriclighting.com

St. Barths Home
303 Broadway
Suite 1041-123
Laguna Beach, CA 92657
800.274.9096
www.stbarthshome.com

Svenska Mobler
154 North Brea Avenue
Los Angeles, CA 90036
www.svenskamobler.com

Swedish Country Interiors
360.570.0876
www.swedishcountry.com

Tara Shaw Antiques
New Orleans Warehouse
1240 Camp Street
New Orleans, LA 70130
504.525.1131
www.tarashaw.com

Tone On Tone Antiques
and Accessories
7920 Woodmont Avenue
Bethesda, MD 20814
240.497.0800
www.tone-on-tone.com

Weinberg Modern
200 Lexington Avenue, Suite 407
New York, NY 10016
646.291.2059
www.weinbergmodern.com

Wisteria
6500 Cedar Springs Road, Suite 100
Dallas, TX 75235
214.350.3115
800.320.9757
www.wisteria.com

CULTURAL ORGANIZATIONS AND MUSEUMS

The American Scandinavian Foundation Scandinavia House
58 Park Avenue @ 38th Street
New York, NY 10016
212.879.9779
info@amscan.org
www.scandinaviahouse.org

The American Swedish Institute
2600 Park Avenue
Minneapolis, MN 55407
612.871.4907
www.americanswedishinst.org

House of Sweden
2900 Street NW and 29th Street NW
Washington, D.C.
202.536.1500
www.houseofsweden.com

Nordic Heritage Museum
3014 NW 67th Street
Seattle, WA 98117
206.789.5707
www.nordicmuseum.org

Swedish American Museum Center
5211 North Clark Street
Chicago, IL 60640
773.728.8111
www.samac.org

Ten Chimneys Foundation
P.O. Box 225
S43 W31575 Depot Road
Genesee Depot, WI 53127
262.968.4161
Tour Reservations:
262.968.4110
www.tenchimneys.org

OTHER

Artisan
Restaurant, tavern, garden
275 Old Post Road
Southport, CT
203.307.4222
www.artisansouthport.com

L. George Walker Appraisals
Jane Edwards, accredited appraiser
    specializing in European
    and Scandinavian antiques
    and decorative arts
203.510.4469
lgeorgewalker@earthlink.net

Acknowledgments

Sometimes you need someone to believe in you. Van Bernhard, thank you for not only believing in this book and in Eleish van Breems, but for propelling us to new skies we had never dreamed imaginable. *Reflections on Swedish Interiors* could not have happened without you!

Thank you to our amazing team at Gibbs Smith, Publisher, especially to Gibbs Smith and Suzanne Taylor for your unfailing support of our books as well as the Scandinavian design movement afoot in America. Hollie Keith, you are the most generous and visionary editor and we are so lucky that you were able to step in to make a reality of what Jennifer Adams had so lovingly shepherded for us. Thank you to the talented Sheryl Dickert for your dedication and book design.

Neil Landino, photographic alchemist, you have transformed our original vision of a book called *Reflections on Swedish Interiors* into poetry with seemingly little more than light and camera. How do you do it? We cannot imagine a more patient, good-humored, talented and tireless partner and we have been so blessed to work on this project with you. This book is yours!

Two gentlemen we admire so very much are Brad Ford and Keith Granet. Many thanks to you both for such generous and personal forewords to this book, as well as for the continued inspiration and wonderful guidance we always look to you for.

Reflections on Swedish Interiors has been a delightful project in which we have been able to share a very personal glimpse into the lives of some of our favorite designers and collectors. We want to thank each and all of them for opening their homes to us, for without their kindness and generosity, this book would not have been possible.

To our dear friend, Jane Edwards, who came to our side and helped to compile the resource guide for this book on such short notice—your help was invaluable and we are so grateful!

Many, many thanks to Laurie Stockwell, Paul Scionti and Arie den Breems for keeping us in order at Eleish van Breems during the course of the writing and producing of this book. Thanks also to Don Lawson and Matt Wood for all of their help during this project.

Rhonda would like to personally thank her parents, artist G. Eleish and Cathy Eleish, as well as her daughter Kari Ergmann, sister P. Eleish and her family, Buffer Ergmann, the Elliots and the Dittus'. Many thanks to Lillian August, Dan and John Weiss, Skye Kirby Westcott and all the teams at Lillian August Designs, Inc. at Knight Street, South Norwalk, Stamford, and New York. Many thanks to Chris Zaima for his beautiful floral arrangements for Duck Pond.

Edie would like to personally thank all her dear family and friends for each listening and supporting her so lovingly during the production of this book. For her sons, Martin and Lars, she will continue to tirelessly pitch the book, *Sail to Bali: A Photographic Journey.* To Paul, she devotes each grammatical error with love.

Rhonda Eleish & Edie van Breems

Rhonda Eleish and Edie van Breems are the founders of Eleish van Breems Ltd., a company whose approach to design stems from a modern application and interpretation of historic Scandinavian interiors and form. They are sought out for their clean, elegant, and fresh approach to interiors, all with a Scandinavian essence. Rhonda and Edie are the authors of *Swedish Interiors* and *Swedish Country Interiors* and are excited to introduce *Reflections on Swedish Interiors* as the third book in their best-selling Swedish Interiors series. Their design work has been featured in fine national and international publications such as *House Beautiful, Elle Decor, Veranda, Glamour, Country Living, Gods & Goddar,* and the *New York Times,* among others. The pair have made television appearances on *This Old House, Martha Stewart Living* and *HGTV-Canada*. Both Rhonda and Edie live with their families in southwest Connecticut and travel extensively in Scandinavia, calling Stockholm their home away from home.

Neil Landino

As a photographer, Neil Landino's work has him travelling for commercial and editorial shoots around the country as well as focusing on private events close to his studio in Fairfield, Connecticut. "I've always enjoyed lines and composition. It wasn't until I put my hands on an SLR film camera that I truly felt that I found the medium that's right for me. When photographing a space, a building, a person, I want my clients to see what I feel, I want to bring out the calmness and emotion of natural light." Neil›s work has been in national, international and regional publications such as HGTV, *Veranda, Connecticut Cottages & Gardens,* and *New York Cottages & Gardens,* as well as featured on countless design websites and blogs. His garden and landscape images are prominently featured in the 2013 book of Doyle Herman Design Associates Landscape designs.